THE 7 UNIVERSAL LAWS

The Hidden Rules Behind the Mind, Emotions, and the Architecture of the Universe

MONICA ION AND STEFAN IRIMIA

ISBNs
eBook: 979-8-9930982-1-0
Paperback: 979-8-9930982-0-3
Hardcover: 979-8-9930982-2-7

TABLE OF CONTENTS

THINGS TO KNOW
BEFORE YOU START

Why 7 Universal Laws

Universal laws are fundamental principles that are known to govern the structure and behavior of the universe. They have withstood the test of time and, as far as we know, apply universally—from tiny subatomic particles to vast clusters of galaxies. They are seen as constant, unchanging, and applicable to all things, regardless of time or space.

Unlike opinions, cultural beliefs, or historical trends, the laws of the universe are unbiased. That's why they provide the most reliable foundation for one's thinking. Building your understanding on such a strong foundation gives you clarity and certainty in a world full of noise and contradiction.

Different disciplines—such as physics, metaphysics, and mathematics—identify various universal laws, like Newton's laws, the law of conservation of energy, the laws of thermo-dynamics, and more.

As you delve into this book, you'll discover that I use only 7 universal laws out of many: the law of duality, the law of reflection, the law of transformation, the law of synchronicity, the law of eristic escalation, the law of order, and the law of fractals. The first 3 chapters cover the law of duality—what it is, how we see it in action, and how it is evidenced across history and across disciplines. This is because the law of duality is the most fundamental—it echoes through every other law. After that, each chapter focuses on one law, offering both theory and real-life stories.

In my work, I found that these 7 universal laws are the most relevant to understanding how the mind operates and to creating transformation in the lives of our clients. Practically speaking, any problem encountered in the physical world can be addressed using these 7 universal laws. While there are many other laws, these 7 are sufficient in the FTP methodology[1] to explain the world as it is, resolve challenges, remove obstacles, and assist clients in achieving their goals. They provide a clear understanding of reality as it is—not as we wish it to be.

My mission is not to prove these laws, nor to teach them. My mission is to solve problems using the universal laws. This focus sets us apart from others who work with similar principles. Some clients have come to us after working with other experts. They've had profound learnings and "aha" moments, but their problems remain unresolved. Our work goes beyond understanding—it's about resolution.

This book doesn't aim to prove the laws either, but to explain them from multiple angles—using analogies and metaphors to support your mind and make connections. At times, I've

---

1 FTP stands for Fast Transformation Protocols—an alternative methodology to coaching and therapy that applies the universal laws of math and physics to human behavior.

taken complex scientific ideas and simplified them boldly, not to meet academic standards, but to make them accessible. Also, key ideas are expressed in several ways to make them easier to grasp, even at the risk of repetition.

This is a simple introduction to the universal laws applied to human behavior and is far from being all-encompassing. In some instances, I merely scratch the surface.[2] It provides enough insight, however, to spark ideas about what's possible, the types of problems you can solve, and the kinds of results you can achieve.

If you want to effectively apply the universal laws to real-life challenges, it will require dedicated practice over time and more advanced training. Even so, I'm confident this book can ignite a powerful shift in perspective for those who are ready. It has the potential to transform your worldview, making it impossible to see things the way you did before.

Real Stories, Fake Names

All the stories in this book are based on real events. They come from cases I have personally worked on over the past decade or more, as well as cases handled by other FTP specialists who have trained with me. Between 2016 and 2023, I logged more than 15,000 hours of one-on-one paid sessions with clients—all thoroughly documented.

---

2   Some readers may find stories and concepts in this book challenging, likely because we've only scratched the surface of the universal laws. Each law and chapter could easily be expanded into a book of its own. So, if you come across something you disagree with, keep in mind that the purpose isn't to provide an in-depth demonstration but to serve as an introduction to the ideas.

To protect client confidentiality, most names in these stories have been changed. Some clients preferred to keep their real names in the stories. Occasionally we've also adjusted certain details to ensure clients cannot be identified. This reflects our team's commitment to respecting privacy.

2 Authors, One Voice

In our household—like many others—the man gets the last word: "Yes, dear, you're right!" All jokes aside, this book is a collaboration between my husband, Stefan, and me, Monica, but we chose to present it in my voice alone, for clarity and ease. Still, what you'll read reflects both of us. Together we have researched and applied the universal laws for more than 12 years. May the ideas here light a path toward greater understanding—for your own journey and for those who walk beside you.

MONICA'S JOURNEY INTO THE UNIVERSAL LAWS

If you're on a journey to find God, have questions as your travel companions.

— Anonymous

I grew up as a highly perceptive child, who sensed things that childhood innocence is meant to shield us from: the quiet fractures in a conversation, the tension humming beneath polite smiles, the unspoken emotions that could fill a room more densely than thick smoke. I felt the awkwardness of what wasn't said, the heavy pauses—especially with my parents. I would often step into a room and immediately sense if something was off, even when everyone else pretended it was fine.

As a child, the world didn't make sense to me. What I was feeling and what adults were saying didn't align. The words they spoke often clashed with what I knew inside to be true. I didn't understand which voice to trust. What was the truth? What were the rules? The way relationships worked, the things people prioritized, the principles they said guided them—none of it followed a logic I could grasp. It felt as if I was operating on another frequency, while the rest of the world moved in a parallel reality with its own inexplicable rules.

I remember one specific moment with my dad. He asked a question, and I knew—without a doubt—what he truly meant, even though I was too young to understand it practically. I could sense the subtext, the underlying need and fear behind his words. I knew exactly what answer he wanted to hear to bring calm to the situation, and I gave it to him. Moments like these happened often, where I felt the weight of unspoken truths but struggled to reconcile them with the surface reality.

In kindergarten, the world overwhelmed me. Everything was too bright, too loud, too unpredictable. My emotions weren't small and contained like the other children's—they crashed over me, unfiltered and immense. The teachers called me "sensitive." They said I needed to toughen up, to learn to let things go. But how do you let go of something that is inside you? My mother, exhausted by my outbursts, took me to a doctor.

"She crumbles at the smallest upset," she told him, exasperation seeping into her voice. "She cries all the time. She blows every minor issue out of proportion. I need something to help her calm down. She's too intense."

The doctor studied me for a few moments before shaking his head. "She feels her emotions deeply," he said. "That's not something to fix." I understood the conversation even though I was too young, physically, to grasp it. That moment stayed with me as a small insight of who I was.

My mother thanked him with a polite nod, but I could tell she wasn't satisfied. We stepped out into the noisy street. We walked to the bus stop in silence, her grip on my hand just a little too tight. On the ride home, I watched her reflection in the window—her eyes distant, her mouth set in a straight line. She didn't look at me, but I felt her disappointment hanging between us, heavy and unspoken. I pressed my forehead to the glass, wishing I could be whatever it was she wanted.

So I made myself smaller. I pulled my emotions inward and packed them tightly inside me, like delicate things wrapped in newspaper and shoved into a box that would not be opened anytime soon. I learned to observe instead of speak. I learned to give people the answers they wanted instead of the truths they did not. I became a perfect mirror, reflecting back only what was safe and socially acceptable.

During my school years, I couldn't fully understand the dynamics between my parents, my classmates, or anyone else. Why were some people liked and others not? Why did my words provoke reactions that made no sense to me? One thing I clearly understood was that my parents valued my academic success—so I threw myself into studying. It became my refuge. I loved solving math problems.

Early in high school, I was so drawn to math that I asked my parents for private tutoring—not for support, but for the love of learning more. I was already imagining myself as a math teacher.

My math tutor welcomed me with a different tone one afternoon. "I just got the IQ test results," she said, looking at me with a serious expression on her face. "147. Impressive." I hadn't thought much about the test she had given me the week before. "IQ test? I'm not even sure what that means," I admitted.

She sat back, her eyes steady. "It means you've got a real knack for numbers, and are very good at problem-solving and abstract thinking. Have you ever thought about pursuing a career in math?"

Her words came as a confirmation of my hidden thoughts; it felt good to be acknowledged for doing something well, after years of carrying the overwhelming sense that I was too much, too complicated. So I continued preparing to become a math teacher, dedicating myself intensively to this goal until the end of high school.

At the last moment, however, I changed my mind and chose to study psychology and sociology, blending my love for numbers with my desire to understand people and my own emotions. Despite my high IQ, deep down I felt stupid and incapable of understanding how the world worked.

I enrolled at the largest university in the country, but even with the prestige of the institution, what I found there was limited. I still didn't get the answers I was seeking. The most important thing I did learn was how to conduct unbiased research, a skill that would later become essential to my journey.

Studying at university didn't make life any less confusing. In fact, the more I thought about it, the more my last name, *Ion*, felt like a sign. An ion is a charged particle—imbalance in search of balance. And that's exactly what my life felt like: a constant push and pull, searching for truth, but never quite getting there.

By my mid-twenties, the search only deepened. I wanted answers—needed them. It wasn't just about understanding myself, but about making sense of all the contradictions around me—the suffering, the chaos. There's an anonymous quote I love: "If you want to find God, have questions as your travel companions." I wasn't looking for God, per se, but I was searching for something—a higher order, a framework to explain the chaos, a meaningful way to make sense of it all.

My spiritual definition of a question is "an ion on a quest"[3] (quest-ion). And that's what I was: a charged particle searching for something—anything—that would make sense of the tension I carried. The quest for meaning in conflict, in suffering, was slow and painful—a puzzle I couldn't solve no matter how many pieces I turned over in my hands.

Yet, despite this, something strange began to happen: people entrusted me with their most private truths. They shared things they hadn't shared with anyone else— worries, regrets, the quiet griefs they carried. I didn't know why they trusted me. I only knew how to listen, and I was feeling their pain like it was my own. I wanted to help, but I didn't know how.

Launching my first company in 2005 became an important stepping stone to discovering my calling and arriving where

---

3   This statement plays on the word *question*, splitting it into *quest* and *ion*, and metaphorically describes curiosity and inquiry as a dynamic process—much like an ion seeking balance or connection. The wordplay was coined by Dr. John Demartini.

I am today. My startup was a recruitment agency for corporations in Transylvania, and it became the largest in the region within a few years. And no, despite what everyone loved to joke about, we weren't in the business of recruiting vampires. What we did was match people with roles in major companies, offering corporate training along the way. It was my first real introduction to personal and professional development. I hadn't expected to find myself in that world, but maybe, in a way, it had found me first.

To teach others, I first had some learning to do myself. I had the rare privilege of finding and working with some of the greatest minds on the planet, being mentored by those who understood the hidden architecture of human behavior.[4] They revealed to me the universal laws that shape both the cosmos and the human experience.

It was a turning point. For the first time, I saw it: an underlying structure to what had always felt like chaos. A mathematical harmony woven into life itself. The same principles that governed the movement of planets, the patterns of nature, the balance of equations—they applied to people, too. Human dynamics, relationships, even suffering—they weren't random. There was an order to it all, one that could be understood, one that could be worked with instead of fought against. It was the first time the world started to make sense to me.

---

4   One mentor I deeply appreciate is Dr. John Demartini. If I were to acknowledge every time something in this book stems from our conversations or his teachings, I'd have to reference him every 5 pages—or even more frequently. Much of what I've learned from him came through direct interactions, which makes it difficult to pinpoint exact references, yet his immense influence has profoundly impacted my thinking overall.

I began applying these insights in my own life, testing them, refining them. And then, one day, I applied them on a friend and colleague named Sara. I'll share her story in chapter 1. By asking the right questions, she was able to unlock something that had been holding her back for years. Her transformation was profound, and so was mine. For the first time, I felt true fulfillment. This moment revealed my life's purpose. My journey was no longer just about making sense of the world for myself—it was about guiding others through their own quests for meaning.

Since childhood, I had felt a deep calling to serve, to be there for people who were going through tough times. But for so long, I had no idea how. I could listen, I could care, but I couldn't change anything. Now, for the first time, I had the tools. Supporting others to find clarity and transformation became my calling. Everything I had done up to that point—the studying, the business successes, the personal struggles—had been preparing me for this.

The years that followed were a whirlwind of work and growth. I found myself immersed in one-on-one sessions, often working 12 to 14 hours a day. I thrived on the intensity because I loved what I was doing. By the time I considered slowing down, the world was in lockdown for COVID-19, and the demand for support skyrocketed. I didn't want to turn people away. As a result, I conducted more than 15,000 paid sessions with individuals between 2016 and 2023. The sheer volume of clients meant I never needed to market myself—referrals kept coming, and the waiting list stretched from 3 to 6 months, even as I steadily raised my rates.

Recognizing the growing demand, I created the first group programs in 2020, which turned out to be an important step forward. These programs expanded over the years, and other professionals joined me in delivering them. The decision wasn't just about scaling my work—it was rooted in something deeper. After spending thousands of hours with clients, I began to notice patterns. I realized I could create protocols to address specific issues. My early dream of being a math teacher resurfaced as I channeled my love for patterns and processes into developing these protocols.

These weren't just theories or ideas—they were repeatable steps that guaranteed results. My work isn't about delivering fleeting "aha" moments or offering a space for exploration, as often happens in coaching or psychotherapy. My focus is on producing tangible results. If there's one thing I want people to say about me, it's this: "Monica's protocols get you results."

Defining my role was a challenge. I didn't want to call myself a coach because coaching often lacks structure and predictable outcomes. I studied psychology and sociology in college, but I avoided titles like *psychologist* or *psychotherapist* because my work went beyond conventional methods. I wasn't interested in being defined by any approach I'd studied, as my practice integrated the laws of math and physics with psychology and spirituality. Eventually, I named my approach Fast Transformation Protocols (FTP). This methodology is about achieving inner transformation and alignment that leads to external results. It's built on repeatable processes that produce consistent outcomes, much like the laws of physics but applied to human behavior. And, true to its name, it's fast—unlike conventional therapy, it doesn't take years to work through recurring issues. With FTP problems are resolved in just a few hours, with lasting results.

Over time, I began certifying others to become FTP specialists. The protocols I developed became the foundation for a growing guild of practitioners who shared my vision of delivering fast, transformative results.

To further expand on this vision, I co-founded Inspired Life Circle, a company dedicated to amplifying the reach and impact of the FTP methodology. Inspired Life Circle serves as a hub for education, community, and resources that support both practitioners and individuals in achieving transformative results. It's not just about teaching transformation protocols—it's about creating a vibrant ecosystem that cultivates connection, growth, and self-mastery on a deeper level.

Somewhere along this journey, I discovered the work of another mentor of mine, Alain Cardon. A friend encouraged me to explore his coaching school, but I initially resisted. I didn't feel the need for another tool—my clients were already getting results. However, an article Alain wrote about quantum physics and coaching caught my attention. It revealed a higher level of order that intrigued me. I decided to approach his teachings with a beginner's mind, setting aside everything I thought I knew.

This decision led me to integrate the law of fractals into my work. The concept is simple yet profound: change the fractal, and you change everything. The last chapter of this book will delve into how the law of fractals can be used to transform not only your life, but also the lives of those around you.

I mention this to make it clear that I didn't invent all these concepts myself. I learned about the universal laws from mentors, who also had learned them from others. As Newton famously said, "If I have seen further, it is by standing on the shoulders of giants."[5] My contribution has been to organize this knowledge into specific forms like books, programs, and especially protocols—a specific sequence of steps—that solve problems and deliver results. There is a specific protocol for each problem you may want to solve and for each result you may want to achieve.

Looking ahead, my vision is that every home and workplace will have someone who understands the universal laws and knows how to ask the right questions to solve painful problems and achieve meaningful goals. Imagine a world where people have the tools to face internal challenges with clarity and confidence—where families and teams resolve conflicts and reach their goals with grace.

The protocols I've developed and the community we're building at Inspired Life Circle are just the beginning. My intention is that through the Fast Transformation Protocols, more people will find the tools they need to transform their lives and, in doing so, inspire others to do the same.

---

5 This statement is from a letter Sir Isaac Newton wrote to fellow scientist Robert Hooke in 1675. The phrase is commonly interpreted as Newton acknowledging the contributions of those who came before him, emphasizing that his groundbreaking discoveries were built upon the knowledge and work of earlier thinkers.

CHAPTER 1

THE LAW OF DUALITY

What opposes unites; the finest harmony stems from things held in tension. All things come into existence through conflict of opposites.

— Heraclitus

Weird Questions

Many years ago, when I was running my recruiting and training company, one of my most important clients was the largest bank in Transylvania. Every month, I would pack my bags and set off on a journey across the country, visiting their various branches and offices.

These trips were far from ordinary, thanks to Sara—our company's cheerful event coordinator. Sara wasn't just responsible for handling logistics—she became my steadfast travel companion. From organizing transport to ensuring every detail was seamless, she had a knack for making even the most chaotic days feel manageable. Over time, our professional partnership evolved into a camaraderie rooted in shared experiences on the road.

On one particular trip we found ourselves crossing the Transylvanian mountains, a breathtaking region that moved me beyond words. The winding roads, framed by dense forests and snow-capped peaks, seemed to inspire deeper conversations. Sara, typically upbeat but reserved, began to open up.

"You know, Monica," she began, her voice soft yet steady, "there's something I've never told anyone at work." I glanced at her, sensing this was significant. "I'm here to listen," I assured her, feeling a spark of curiosity stirring within me. What was she about to tell me?

She took a deep breath. "When I was in sixth grade, my family hit a financial crisis. My mom made the hardest decision of her life. She left us and went abroad to work so she could send money back home."

"That must have been incredibly tough for all of you," I empathized, sensing how much it had affected her. Her breath was shallow and her eyes were brimming with tears.

Sara nodded, turning her gaze to the passing scenery. "It was. My dad... he wasn't stable. He had mental health issues and drank heavily. It was a nightmare. I never knew what to expect when I came home. Would he be drunk? Would the house be a mess? It didn't feel like home at all." She paused before adding, "I had to grow up fast. At school I was bullied for being too quiet, for wearing secondhand clothes, for always looking exhausted. At home I had to be the adult and keep it together. It was overwhelming."

"How did you cope with all of that?" I asked, my voice barely above a whisper, feeling the weight of her struggle.

"I didn't—not really," she admitted. "Even as an adult, I carried the pain. I went to therapy for years. CBT, EMDR, Theta Healing, Reiki—you name it. But nothing worked. The pain was still there." For a moment, I just sat there, connecting with what she had been carrying. I could deeply feel what she told me. I took a deep breath and decided to share something that had helped me in my own life. "Sara, have you ever heard of the law of duality?"

She gave me a puzzled look. "No, what is it?"

"It's about finding balance," I explained. "For every challenge, there's a benefit—even if it's hard to see at first. Let's try something. What are some of the benefits of your mother's decision to leave?" Her jaw clenched, and a flicker of tension tightened the skin around her eyes. "Benefits? Monica, my mother abandoned me."

"I understand why it feels that way," I said gently, not wanting her to shut down. I explained that "abandonment" is a label, not the action her mother actually did. What did her mother do? She went to work abroad and left Sara at home with her emotionally unstable father.

Reluctantly, she began. Her voice had an edge now, sharp but controlled, like she was keeping a dam from breaking. "Well, we didn't lose the house. We had food on the table."

"Great start," I encouraged her. I could see the effort behind it, the way she reached for the words despite the difficulty.

"Now, what might have been the disadvantages if she had stayed?" Sara hesitated but eventually answered, "We might have been evicted. My dad... he wouldn't have managed to keep us afloat."

We went back and forth, answering these questions: "What were the benefits of your mother leaving?" and "What would have been the drawbacks if she had stayed?" At first, the process felt strange to her. "These questions are so weird," she said with a nervous laugh. "But I'll keep going."

At one point, a deep silence filled the car. No one spoke. I could sense she was processing everything we had discussed. In that quiet moment, I knew something within her was realigning.

She sat in the passenger seat, silent, deeply absorbed in thought. She didn't cry or have any emotional outbursts, but I could sense something shifting within her. It reminded me of my own experiences—those moments of internal transformation when something deconstructs and reconstructs simultaneously, like a profound reorganization of information happening throughout my entire being, not just in my mind.

So, I let the silence be and work its magic. Silence can be healing, and in that moment any words would have been a distraction. Half an hour passed without a word.

Two weeks later I met Sara again at a gas station, ready for another trip. As I stood outside, the distinct smell of fuel filled the air. The moment she saw me she ran into my arms, her entire presence radiating joy. She looked completely different—light, free, transformed. With a beaming smile, she said, "Thank you so much, Monica! You helped me resolve in 1 hour what I couldn't in years of therapy."

Seeing her face, feeling her energy, and witnessing the change she had undergone, I had a realization: this is what I'm meant to do. Nothing I had ever done before gave me the certainty that it was worth dedicating my entire life to—until that moment. It was life-changing. That was when I made the decision: I would pursue the certifications I needed, travel wherever necessary, and invest whatever it took to do this work of transformation.

Many times, transformation starts with questions that seem weird—simply because you hadn't considered them before. In Sara's case, we toggled between *What were the benefits?* and *What were the drawbacks?* In this and other chapters, you'll find questions designed to help you experience each universal law from the inside out.

Definition of the Law of Duality

The law of duality states that

the whole is made up of complementary opposites.

Everything that we can perceive through our senses exists in pairs of opposites. Just as there is day and night, there is also good and evil, order and chaos, yin and yang. These are not contradictions but complementary forces that create balance and harmony.

When I first learned about the law of duality, the world finally started making sense to me.

Since I was a child, I had observed that society was not congruent. Deep in my heart, I felt that something was not right with the grown-ups, but I didn't know what. I heard my parents and teachers saying things like, "Be happy. Don't be sad. Feel confident. Don't be hesitant. Be generous. Don't be stingy. Be nice. Don't be mean." Yet they would do exactly the opposite of what they said. They often felt sad, they doubted themselves, they did not give generously, and they were mean to each other.

My intuition kept whispering to me that striving for one side without integrating the other was pointless. Trying to be one-sided felt as impossible as trying to separate one side of a magnet from the other. No matter how hard you try, you can never achieve it.

Will Durant (1885–1981), the American historian and philosopher known for *The Story of Civilization*, spent his life studying the rise and fall of human societies. In *The Story of Philosophy*, he explores Hegel's concept of development through opposing forces—thesis, antithesis, and synthesis—describing it as central to historical and philosophical progress: "Of all relations, the most universal is that of contrast or opposition. Every condition of thought or of things—every idea and every situation in the world—leads irresistibly to its opposite, and then unites with it to form a higher or more complex whole. [...] The movement of evolution is a continuous development of oppositions and their merging and reconciliation. [...] Thesis, antithesis and synthesis constitute the formula and secret of all development and all reality."[6]

---

6   Will Durant, *The Story of Philosophy: The Lives and Opinions of the Greater Philosophers* (Simon and Schuster, 1926), 275–76.

What Comes Before Your Thoughts and Emotions

Let's explore how the mind works and start with the fundamentals.

Before we take any action, before we make a decision, and before we even think, there is something else that goes on in the human mind. Have you ever wondered how you process the world around you? How your mind is turning raw data into meaningful experiences? This process can be broken down into 4 key stages: stimulus, sensations, perceptions, and emotions. Let's explore each step.

1. Stimulus: The Beginning of Experience

A stimulus is any external factor that activates our senses—such as light, sound, smell, taste, or touch. For example, the sound of music or the sight of a sunrise triggers this process. Stimuli are the starting point for how we interact with our environment.

2. Sensations: Collecting Raw Data

When a stimulus is detected, our sensory organs (eyes, ears, skin, etc.) collect raw information and send it to the brain. This stage, known as sensation, is where the mind gathers data about the environment.

For instance, light waves hitting your eyes create the sensation of brightness, and sound waves vibrating your eardrums produce the sensation of noise.

Sensations on their own are merely signals—they don't yet have any meaning.

3. Perceptions: The Interpretation and Meaning

The brain processes these sensations into perceptions, assigning meaning to the raw data. Perception is influenced by memory, past experiences, and the context of the situation.

For example, the bright light you see might be perceived as a beautiful sunrise, and the noise you hear might be recognized as your favorite song.

This stage allows us to understand what's happening and prepares us for the next step: our emotional reaction.

4. Emotions: Responding to Meaning

Once we perceive a situation, emotions emerge in response to the meaning we assign. Emotions shape how we react to the stimulus.

For example, if sunrise is something you perceive as beautiful, you may feel calm or joyful, and if the noise you hear reminds you of a happy memory, you might feel nostalgic.

Emotions act as a guide, helping us make decisions and interact with our environment.

What This Looks Like in Practice

Imagine you're walking in a park and hear rustling in the bushes:

1. **Stimulus**: Leaves are crushed underfoot.

2. **Sensation**: Your ears detect the sound.

3. **Perception**: You interpret it as a big animal moving and a potential threat.

4. **Emotion**: You feel fear and you become alert. You are now ready to run or defend yourself.

But, after 2 seconds the cutest puppy jumps out of the bushes, looks at you with its big wet eyes and your heart melts. You don't want to run anymore. Now, you want to get closer and pet that bundle of joy.

In this process, perception is key. Perception is the interpretation of the stimulus and it impacts everything. It impacts your emotions, your thoughts, and your actions—short-term and long-term.

To go a layer deeper, consider this: the event, the leaves being crushed, is neutral. Only at the perception level do you interpret it as positive or negative, harmless or harmful.

Now, let's consider the puppy as a stimulus, or an event. Seeing the puppy is neutral. If your interpretation is that the puppy wants to play, you will experience a particular set of emotions. If your interpretation is that the puppy might be sick or injured, you will experience another type of emotions. If your interpretation is that the puppy looks like the dog who bit you when you were a child, you will probably experience a very different set of emotions. And I could go on and on with possible perceptions or interpretations that will clearly lead to different emotions, thoughts, and actions.

In my opinion, modern psychology overlooks how crucial perception truly is and even worse, it does not consider perception as a key factor of the therapeutic process. Similar to how healthcare prioritizes symptoms over underlying conditions, there is much more emphasis on elements like emotions, memory, attention, or decisions instead of their origin.

The ancient philosophers understood this. Almost 2000 years ago, Epictetus said that "man is disturbed not by things (stimulus), but by the views he takes of them (perception)."[7] In other words, it's not what happens to you (the event), but how you react to it (interpretation) that matters.

In more recent history, Holocaust survivor and Austrian neurologist Viktor Frankl wrote that "the last of the human freedoms" is the ability to choose one's own path, even in the darkest of times.[8] Paraphrasing Frankl's experience, Stephen Covey beautifully said that "between stimulus and response, there is a space. In that space lies our power to choose our response. In our response lies our growth and our freedom."[9] Frankl is a man who witnessed some of the worst things you can imagine, and yet he highlights the power of perception or interpretation. We see that power of perception in Sara's story, who was able to give a different meaning to her experience and go through an extraordinary transformation because of it.

In my work at Inspired Life Circle, we focus on perceptions as the key point that impacts our inner world. That's why I say we act upon the root cause, because perception is the first stage where your mind has control.

---

7 Epictetus, *The Handbook (Enchiridion)*, trans. Nicholas P. White (Hackett Publishing, 1983), sec. 5. Parenthetical statements added.

8 Viktor E. Frankl, *Man's Search for Meaning*, trans. Ilse Lasch (Beacon Press, 2006), 65.

9 Stephen R. Covey, A. Roger Merrill, and Rebecca R. Merrill, *First Things First* (Simon & Schuster, 1994), 70.

First Question to Apply the Law of Duality: *What Are the Benefits?*

Five years ago, I worked with an entrepreneur named Lois who was upset that her husband was financially dependent on her. She built her business on her own and was well respected in her community, carrying herself with the assurance of a woman who relied on no one. Her husband, however, had previously owned a business and stopped working altogether after closing it down. This situation caused her significant distress.

Every week, as Lois made payments to employees and suppliers, she was reminded that her husband was not making any financial contributions to the family's well-being. Instead, she had to support him financially as well.

When they would meet people at events they attended together, the conversation would sometimes turn to business and each person's occupation. Lois felt ashamed that her husband wasn't working, and was troubled by the contrast between his lack of activity and her status in the community.

When she reached out to me, I could sense the mix of frustration and sadness beneath her words. Lois wanted to understand why this situation affected her so deeply, why it stirred feelings of resentment and shame. As I listened, I recognized that this was about more than just money—it was about expectations and the silent struggles we carry in our closest relationships.

So we began by balancing her perceptions, untangling the emotions and beliefs that had shaped her experience.

"What are the benefits of your husband not working? What do you gain from your current situation?" I asked her.

"Benefits?" Lois looked at me incredulously. "There are no benefits. He doesn't contribute at all. I've spent so much money on him just in the last 6 months. How can there possibly be benefits?" Then she went on to tell me the whole story again.

"I understand the question might sound strange, but it's intentional. There's a principle I'd like to share with you in just a bit, called the law of duality. For now, just answer my question, please. What are some benefits, even small ones, that come from him not working?"

Her eyes softened with introspection as she looked up. A slow breath followed, like she was gently unpacking long-held memories. "Ok. He drives me to places sometimes. He comes with me on business trips. He does a few small things around the house."

"Great answers. What else?" I asked.

"I don't know. Maybe he's just there—if I need him to do something small, like run an errand." Lois's body remained taut—her shoulders still held a faint rigidity, and her hands fidgeted in her lap.

After she had listed about 30 responses, I confronted her and said: "These answers are correct, but they don't move you. They aren't truly relevant."

"You're right," she admitted.

"What is the real, deeper reason in your heart for which it's worth keeping your husband in this state, financially dependent on you? You haven't divorced him, you've chosen to stay in this relationship. So something about the situation works for you. What is it?"

She tried again to offer some small answers, and I stopped her. Her mind was acting like a cornered little mouse, trying to escape in various directions. After a few seconds of silence, Lois whispered the answer she had been avoiding, "If he depends on me, he can't leave me." Tears welled up in her eyes, the tension in her shoulders easing. "That's it, isn't it? I'm afraid he'll leave." She had just uttered her greatest fear.

"Perfect! Then you've built the best strategy for that, haven't you? You've achieved what truly mattered to you." She nodded, tears streaming down her face, a newfound meaning filling her eyes. "I never thought of it that way."

Her mind became quiet as she perceived the intricate beauty of her inner world and the perfection of her subconscious mind. She left the session peacefully, carrying with her a soft radiance.

Two months later, Lois's husband started a new venture within her business. He effectively launched a new line of business, which he began managing himself, on his own initiative, without her asking or pressuring him to do so.

The Principle of Quantitative and Qualitative Compensation

The principle of quantitative and qualitative compensation is a concept often used in economics, business management, and environmental science. It refers to the idea that any loss, damage, or change in one area should be balanced by providing an appropriate form of compensation that restores equilibrium either in measurable terms (quantitative) and/or in terms of intrinsic value (qualitative).

Quantitative compensation involves replacing the lost amount, or measurable aspects, such as planting an equivalent number of trees for deforestation or offering monetary reimbursement. Qualitative compensation, on the other hand, addresses non-measurable attributes, such as restoring ecological balance or offering professional development to counterbalance reduced job satisfaction. This principle ensures fairness and sustainability by maintaining overall value, whether tangible or intangible.

This is also how the mind works: quantitatively and qualitatively. This is why I train FTP specialists to ask for a sufficient number of answers (quantity) but also look for the ones that really matter (quality).

In the example from the previous section, my entrepreneur client gave about 30 correct answers for the situation she was working on, but not really relevant for her mind. This phase is actually essential because it engages the most advanced part of the brain, the neocortex, moving away from the frustration or pain and beginning to consider alternative perspectives. It makes the mind more flexible—so I often accept small trivial benefits because I know they help.

The qualitative answers are often hidden under layers of quantitative answers. It's like finding a few gems among many pebbles. Once you discover those precious gems—the real benefits—they carry far more weight than any list of smaller, superficial benefits.

Second Question to Apply the Law of Duality:
What Are the Drawbacks of the Ideal Situation?

A few years ago I worked with John, an entrepreneur from Paris. His construction company had finished a project for the French government and they owed him $250,000. But week after week, the notorious French bureaucracy delayed his payment with excuses like "you need to submit another document," or "the manager is away this week, so we can't get the signature," or "the other boss is out now, so we can't get approval."

After a while, the situation became critical. John had no money left to sustain his business. If he didn't get paid soon, he'd be unable to pay his team and suppliers. His business would collapse.

When he came to me, John really wanted to solve this problem. The dark circles under his eyes said it all. I asked him, "What benefits do you gain from not receiving the money?"

He blinked, and his posture shifted. A flicker of frustration crossed his face. "What do you mean, benefits? This is money I worked hard for! They should even pay me interest!"

John's anger didn't surprise me. It was the frustration of feeling wronged. But I knew that beneath it was the real reason he was stuck. So I asked again: "What benefits do you gain from not receiving the money?"

He exhaled sharply, shaking his head. "Benefits?" he repeated in disbelief. He resisted—not me, but the idea that there could be any upside to this situation. I stayed silent, holding his gaze, giving him space to think. Slowly, his expression changed. Instead of anger, I saw concentration. He hesitated, searching for an answer. Then he started listing small benefits.

"I'll finally let go of unproductive employees I should have fired long ago. I'll reorganize the company and become more efficient. I'll cut unnecessary expenses." These weren't really relevant, but it was a sign that John's mind started to become more flexible. Then I asked, "What *drawbacks* would you have if you *received* the money?"

Something clicked. John's eyes widened. "I'd have to buy my wife a car, even though I don't want to. But I promised her I would, once I got paid." I noticed his body relax before he even spoke. His shoulders eased, his jaw unclenched, and his grip on the chair loosened. He had found the answer.

I told him, "Talk to your wife. Share your vision with her." I already knew his vision: accumulate cash, invest, flip houses, and rent them out. He had a clear number of properties in mind.

When clients tell me their plans, I can sense when they are truly aligned with them. If I can picture their plans clearly, I know they're genuine. If not, something is off, and it's more wishful thinking or mere desire than real alignment.

I understood John's struggle. He wanted to stay committed to his vision, but he also felt obligated to keep his promise. So I suggested, "Ask your wife to use the current car for now. Tell her you want to save and invest for 3 years. Then, after 3 years, you'll buy her any car she wants. Ask for her trust and support." He agreed and spoke with her. She understood and supported him wholeheartedly.

Three days later, John called me. "Monica, I can't believe it! The French government sent proof of the transfer. I got the money!"

"That's amazing!" I said.

"I'm stunned. Is this really possible?"

"Did you talk to your wife?" I asked.

"Yes! And it went well. But I can't believe how fast this happened."

"Great. And you received the money today?"

"Yes!"

"Did something shift within you after our session?"

"Definitely."

"You weren't resisting the money—you were resisting what it represented," I said. "You didn't want to buy the car. Once you worked through the real issue, you untangled the entire knot."

John laughed. "You know, I haven't received the full amount yet. I got $225,000 instead of $250,000." He paused. "The missing $25,000? That was for my wife's car." It was funny. The situation was mostly resolved but not completely. He eventually got the remaining $25,000 after fixing some documentation issues.

Like John, you may be wondering how this happened. Initially, John's mind perceived more negatives than positives in receiving the money—which is ultimately why he didn't get it. After balancing his perception, money became neutral, and there was no longer a need to create an external challenge. The way for the money was now open.

Some people call this magic—how things shift when you balance your perceptions. But it's not magic, it's physics. When your mind becomes neutral and balanced, you stop creating the opposing pole. It's logical.

Others call it coincidence. I have many such "coincidences" to share. In this book, I'll break down the logic behind this phenomenon. Since ancient times, masters have understood that inner achievements determine outer reality. For instance, in Plato's *Apology*, Socrates admonishes the Athenians: "Virtue (inner reality) does not come from money (outer reality), but from virtue comes money and all other good things to man, both to the individual and to the state."[10] This is a clear statement that external goods (wealth, benefit in society) flow from the inner state, not the other way around.

When You Can't Find Benefits or Drawbacks by Yourself

Every emotional state that we go through has a different degree of intensity, positive or negative. We call this intensity *charge*, like in physics. A positive charge is associated with emotions that feel pleasant—like happiness, joy, or excitement. A negative charge is associated with emotions that feel unpleasant—like sadness, anger, or fear.

---

10 Plato, *Apology*, in *The Trial and Death of Socrates: Four Dialogues*, trans. Benjamin Jowett (Dover Publications, 1992), 29b–d. Parenthetical statements added.

Do you remember entering a bakery and the seller smiling at you? The emotion was pleasant but the positive charge was small. You probably didn't spend the whole day thinking about that individual.

But what about when you were a teenager and the most attractive boy or girl in the school smiled at you? You likely spent a lot of time thinking about them, didn't you? That's because the positive charge was higher. You probably couldn't focus on your schoolwork and were mentally absent in conversation with others because your mind was somewhere else.

We also experience negative charges. When you're driving and someone cuts you off, you might get a little frustrated, but after 15 minutes you forget about it. That's a small negative charge.

If your boss criticizes you publicly, however, and their opinion is important to you, you will have a significant negative charge about it. That event will stick with you for a while, and you might even have trouble concentrating because of it. You'll probably replay scenarios in your head, thinking about what you should've said but didn't, and your mind won't be able to settle.

When John came to work with me, you can imagine that he was experiencing a high negative charge about not getting his money from the French government. When the charge is high, everybody will find it difficult to see benefits or drawbacks. The higher the charge, the more difficult it is to balance the mind using the law of duality.

I can tell how charged a client is about an issue when I ask them about the benefits or drawbacks. Sometimes they resist the question so much that they'll say "there's absolutely no benefit," or "there's definitely no drawback." It can take 30 minutes before they come up with even a small one. But then a few more come to them, and their mind starts to loosen up.

When the charge is high, it can be difficult to "see the other side" on your own, and you may need external support to overcome those blind spots. An experienced specialist can hold space for you with the certainty that the other side exists, no matter how challenging the situation may seem. It's like a doctor who knows with confidence that the illness is curable—and their certainty becomes the foundation of your healing.

Third Question to Apply the Law of Duality: *Where Do They Do the Opposite?*

When my daughter, Elena, was about 10 years old, her messiness pushed me over the edge. It wasn't just that she left a trail of things behind her wherever she went—it was that she couldn't see it. If it had been contained to her room, maybe I could have tolerated it. But no—her clutter spilled over into every space I considered mine.

The kitchen counter, where I tried to maintain some semblance of order, became a battlefield of half-finished projects. The living room, my one sanctuary where I longed for stillness, turned into a chaotic mix of books, markers, and crumpled papers. The dining table, meant for family meals, was overtaken by her latest obsession. Even my own bedroom didn't escape her reach.

It wasn't just the mess. It was the constant frustration of picking up after her, tripping over her shoes, only to find her socks abandoned right beside them. No matter how many times I reminded her, it was as if she didn't see the mess. Worse, she didn't seem to notice how hard I was working to keep our home from descending into utter chaos.

With a degree in psychology and sociology, I thought I knew what to do. I understood motivation, so I thought I should have been able to figure this out. I tried every method I could think of.

First, I tried being patient—explaining, showing her how to do it, and even praising her for small efforts. I even resorted to rewarding her, thinking that would work. But nothing shifted.

Then I tried something more forceful—threats. "If you don't clean up, no cartoons for you today," or "You won't be going to your friend's house." I felt myself slipping into a place I didn't want to be, resorting to methods that felt manipulative. It was awful. And none of it worked.

The frustration mounted every day as I walked through the house, tripping over her belongings again and again. The mess never seemed to change, no matter how many times I asked, reminded, or pleaded. And at my lowest, I felt the urge to physically punish her as my parents had done to me. I knew it wouldn't solve anything so I didn't act on it, but it was a sign that I was reaching my tipping point.

I dreaded the thought that if she was like this now, at 10 years old, what would happen when she became a teenager and what kind of arguments we would have then.

So one day, I decided enough was enough. I had to tackle this differently—it was getting under my skin far too much.

I turned to the law of duality, a principle that says for every trait someone shows, they also possess its opposite in equal measure, even if it's hidden. I asked myself, "Where does Elena show the opposite of this behavior? Where does she demonstrate order?"

It wasn't easy at all to find answers because I had a huge judgment about the fact that she wasn't orderly. Fortunately, this charge wasn't so overwhelming that I couldn't work on it on my own.

I realized that in the 4 years she had been in school, she had never forgotten a notebook at home, even though I never checked how she packed her schoolbag. Her teacher had never complained that she forgot to do her homework. She did her homework, didn't forget her notebooks—and managed this all by herself, because I didn't check on her.

Then, I took a step back and asked myself where she demonstrated order in her own space. That's when I saw it: Elena had a small collection of children's makeup items—neatly organized, color-coded, and arranged by category. Nail polish was all in one spot, eyeshadow in another, lipstick perfectly lined up. In that chaos, there was a hidden order—one I hadn't seen because I'd been too focused on her mess.

She also had a set of fancy clothes she had received from abroad, special ones. And those were also orderly and well-kept.

At that time, she was attending ballet classes. It struck me that she hadn't missed any ballet lessons. She was focused.

She packed her ballet equipment herself because she went straight there after school. I didn't have to remind her, "you have ballet today, take your gear with you." She had her ballet equipment with her when she needed to.

So, when it came to the things that were important to her, she was orderly. She had order in her own form, just not in the form that I was expecting.

Do you realize what it means for a child between the ages of 7 and 10 to have that kind of discipline without anyone reminding them—to check their notebooks against the schedule, not confuse days or times, take their equipment when they have ballet, and think about which days they have classes and bring the gear? It's a pretty big deal.

Where I once saw her as the embodiment of messiness, I now realized that she also had a sense of order. Not only that, but I saw that she had order in equal measure to the disorder I had previously perceived.

Two days after I had the realization about her, she tidied up her schoolbag on her own without me having to say a word. She took out her things, got rid of the sandwich forgotten there for 2 weeks, and organized everything.

The next day, she cleaned out her school locker and her room. She did that on her own, without me giving her any directives. And since then, we haven't had a single argument about messiness. That was it.

Contrasts in the Mind

I'm going to say something that will not sit well with some psychologists: we can't perceive anything without contrast.

Contrast is the foundation of perception—without it, the mind has nothing to measure against.

We hear a noise in the bushes—that's the event—and our mind will immediately deem it a threat, although it might just be a puppy. So perception, or interpretation, is a form of judgement. When we automatically judge an event, we apply a label: threat, safe, good, bad, warm, cold, and so on.

Perception, or judgement, is based on contrasts. We can't state what is "cold" if we don't have "hot" as a reference. We can't perceive what is "far away" if we don't have a "close up" reference. We can't perceive what is "loud" if we don't know what "quiet" means.

If you were to find yourself in an infinite white space—nothing but white, like in a dream—you would not be able to orient yourself. If you were to find yourself in complete darkness, it would be similar—you would not be able to orient yourself. If all of a sudden, a black dot appeared in that infinite white, everything would change. Your mind needs contrasts to interpret the outside world, and therefore judgement is based on contrast.

The law of contrast is an important principle in psychology. It was first articulated by the philosopher and psychologist David Hume in the 18th century, and explored further in the 19th century by Wilhelm Wundt, the "father of experimental psychology." There are many scientific studies conducted every day about contrasts—maybe because it impacts many areas of our daily lives, like decision-making, design, education, marketing, and so on.

Contrasts come in pairs of opposites:

- (temperature) warm - cold
- (light) bright - dark
- (texture) soft - rough
- (sound) loud - quiet
- (taste) sweet - bitter
- (touch or pain) sharp - dull
- (smell) fresh - stale
- (speed) fast - slow
- (weight) heavy - light
- (material resistance) hard - soft
- (moisture) wet - dry
- (pitch in sound) high - low
- (surface feel) sticky - slippery
- (volume or capacity) full - empty
- (density or texture) thick - thin
- (visual clarity) clear - blurry
- (surface shape) flat - bumpy
- (concentration) dense - sparse

I could continue with hundreds of similar pairs of opposites, because our entire thinking is based on them.

In the previous story with my daughter, Elena, my judgement was about order and disorder. I perceived my daughter to be messy and I perceived myself to be tidy.

Now let's go a layer deeper and upset some more psychologists. Are you ready?

Whatever you have a *philia* for, you have a *phobia* of its opposite.

and...

Whatever you have a *phobia* of, you also have a *philia* for its opposite.

Philia and *phobia* are Latin words that describe attraction and repulsion: *philia* is an attraction for something, and *phobia* is a repulsion for something. *Philia* and *phobia* come together simultaneously.

When I had a phobia of my daughter's messiness, I had philia for my own tidiness. In other words, I was attracted to my perceived order, and I was repelled by her perceived disorder. And as long as I was in this duality, my mind couldn't be quiet because it was metaphorically pushed and pulled by the forces of attraction and repulsion. That's why my buttons were pushed every day.

To move beyond this duality, I focused on where my daughter displayed the opposite trait. I was resenting her because I perceived just one side—only being messy—like she was an incomplete human. The moment I saw that she displayed both sides, I could see her for who she really was and our dynamic changed. By seeing her as a whole, I moved beyond attraction and repulsion, philia and phobia, and my mind found balance. I no longer oscillated between 2 extremes and the whole dynamic shifted. This understanding sets the stage for deeper applications of the law of duality.

Scarlett Gets Over Her Ex with the Law of Duality

A few years ago, a colleague of mine who was also an FTP specialist had several sessions with a client named Scarlett. Scarlett wanted to process unresolved emotions about her ex-boyfriend. She was still in love with him even though they had broken up 2 years earlier, and she was still suffering.

She thought about him every day. She had tried other relationships over the past 2 years—but it was no surprise they didn't work out, because she was fascinated by someone else. Her ex-boyfriend was placed on a very high pedestal, and she sacrificed her existence before this imaginary altar.

One of the traits she admired and obsessed over was that her ex-boyfriend had strikingly beautiful blue eyes. This is a neutral stimulus or event, just like the rustling in a bush. Both the rustling in a bush and the blue eyes are neutral. The interpretation we give them is what matters.

So the FTP specialist asked her what those blue eyes represented. Scarlett told him they expressed connection, that this man connected with her through his beautiful blue eyes. That was her perception.

The specialist asked, "Okay, what is the opposite of that?" Scarlett replied, "Not having blue eyes." But it's not the external stimulus or event that interests us—it's the interpretation or perception. So the specialist asked again, "What is the opposite of connecting through his blue eyes?" She understood this time and told him the opposite is "being cold and creating distance."

They started looking for moments when that man did the opposite. That is, "When was he cold and created distance through his blue eyes?"

At first, Scarlett didn't want to find answers. In other words, she was both unwilling and unable—it was a mix of the two. Do you remember when you fell in love as a teenager and couldn't see anything negative about that individual? And, if one of your friends happened to criticize the person you were in love with, you would have hit the "unfriend" button immediately—even though social media didn't exist back then.

When we are deeply infatuated with a person or even an idea, we don't see them for who they truly are. We only see one side of that person or concept. This distorted perception pulls the mind to one side more strongly than iron filings are drawn to a magnet. That's why you can't get them out of your mind. That's why you can't focus at work. That's why you can't sleep at night. When you balance the perception, it's as if you deactivate the magnet—by bringing the positive and negative together, they cancel each other out. Your mind becomes free and no longer thinks obsessively in one direction.

So it was no surprise that Scarlett couldn't find the answer to the question, "When was he cold and created distance through his blue eyes?"

The specialist rephrased the question: "When did he give a look that conveyed coldness? When did you feel from his gaze that he conveyed distance and coldness? When was he absent through his gaze and created distance that way?" He kept asking until Scarlett began to recall a moment and said, "Yes, he gave a look then that was clearly meant to push me away."

When she finally found that moment, her mind began to become more flexible. Then there was another pause when she couldn't find answers again. Slowly, slowly, she found another moment, and another, when through his gaze, that man conveyed distance, kept distance, and created distance between them. My colleague and Scarlett continued like this until she saw that her ex-boyfriend had manifested both sides in equal measure, quantitatively and qualitatively. She deactivated the "magnet" in her mind.

Three months after this session, Scarlett wrote to my colleague to say that she was in a new relationship and felt fulfilled. A year later, they got married. She was able to enter that commitment because she could appreciate her partner for who he was without judging him through the lens of the old relationship.

This process may appear to be long and exhausting at first—but in reality, it's the quickest way to resolve mental charges. And once they're resolved, they don't come back. You address the root cause, solving the problem once and for all.

Positive and Negative Charge

Can you tell me exactly what you were doing a year ago on this very day? Take a second and try to answer. Where were you? Who did you meet? What did you accomplish that day? There are 2 possible scenarios: you are either able to answer right away, or you are not. Let's see why.

If you are not able to answer, it's because you don't have memories from that day. If you are able to answer, it's because you do have memories from that day. But what makes the difference? And what makes the memories?

If something significantly positive or something significantly negative happened that day, you remember it.[11] If you don't have intense emotions, you will not.

For instance, if you attended the wedding of your best friend that day, or if your child was born, or you successfully completed an important project, these are positive memories that you will most likely remember. On the other hand, if you had a car accident, if a family member died, or it was 9/11, these are negative memories that you will remember.

When someone is angry or upset about something, we often say they are *charged* about that issue. And you can approximate the level of *charge* in that person depending on how rational or irrational they behaved in that moment.

---

11 The amygdala plays a crucial role in assigning emotional significance, or valence, to stimuli by interacting with the hippocampus. This interaction influences how memories are encoded and later recalled as positive or negative experiences (positive and negative charges). When an emotional event occurs, the amygdala becomes highly active, signaling the hippocampus to strengthen the encoding and consolidation of these memories. This process is facilitated by the release of stress hormones and neurotransmitters, which modulate synaptic plasticity and enhance neural connectivity. Intracranial EEG studies have shown that the amygdala triggers pronounced hippocampal sharp-wave ripples after encoding emotional experiences, further reinforcing the consolidation of these memories during both wakefulness and sleep. This coordinated activity ensures that emotionally significant events are prioritized in long-term memory storage, leveraging both immediate neurochemical changes and enduring structural adaptations in neural circuits. In summary, the amygdala assigns valence to stimuli and interacts with the hippocampus to "tag" memories with a quality, thereby influencing how we remember events as positive or negative.

Using terms from physics, we call a positive memory a positive charge and a negative memory a negative charge. If you don't have a positive or a negative charge, there is no memory. If it is neutral—neither positive nor negative—your mind will not keep it.

Our memories have a great impact on our lives. We carry with us the experiences we had during childhood, 10 years ago, a week ago, and so on. This is the true baggage that is holding us back. It's like an immense weight that is slowing us down and preventing us from moving freely. We're not free to have the relationships we desire, to earn more money, or to seize the right opportunities for our careers or businesses.

What my colleague and Scarlett were able to do in the previous story, is to balance the charge she had regarding her ex-boyfriend's beautiful blue eyes. That charge occupied so much space and time in her mind that she couldn't have a new relationship. When Scarlett saw the other side, plus and minus canceled each other and her memory was freed.

My colleagues and I have worked with many clients on traumatic events and after we assisted them in balancing their perception, they almost couldn't remember the event anymore. Not because it didn't happen, but because there was no charge left. The memory no longer held weight—it was like clearing space on a hard drive. They were free.

Life relies on electrical activity. That means positive and negative charges. If the body completely loses its electrical activity, it means death. The heart relies on electrical signals to beat. The nervous system uses electrical impulses to transmit signals between neurons. Cells maintain electrical gradients, or membrane potentials, which are essential for functions like nutrient transport and signal transmission.

Why do we assume the inner world is any different? Positive and negative, plus and minus—these 2 poles shape both the outer and the inner world.

When you release an internal charge, it often reflects on the external reality. The person who owed you money finally makes the payment. The individual who was suing you suddenly backs down and withdraws their claims. Or out of nowhere your teenager tidies up their room for the first time, without being asked. A skeptic might dismiss these events as mere coincidences, claiming there's no connection between the inner work and the outer outcomes—it just happened.

On the other side of the spectrum, there are people who see connections everywhere, even if there are no connections. They might interpret unrelated events as signs or patterns, weaving intricate narratives where they don't exist.

When you do the work, complete the process, and release the inner charge, you reach a state of certainty and gratitude. It's easy to analyze, form opinions, or theorize without actually doing the work—but that approach can only take you so far. Just as no amount of intellectual explanation can truly capture the experience of falling in love, some things can only be grasped when you do the work yourself.

Practical Application

You've likely wondered how to apply this in real life and work with your perceptions. Here are 2 ways to get started.

1. Neutralize a Mild Charge on Your Own

Choose a recent action by another person that irritated you and seemed to have more drawbacks than benefits. I suggest you pick something with medium intensity, like 4 or 5 on a scale of 1 to 10. Here are just a few examples to inspire you:

- A colleague interrupted you during a meeting and you felt dismissed.
- You received unexpected criticism from a client and couldn't stop thinking about it.
- Your partner forgot something important to you, and you felt unappreciated.
- A friend didn't reply to your message, and you felt ignored.
- Someone cut you off in traffic, and it triggered a disproportionate reaction.
- Somebody excluded you from a group conversation or decision.
- Somebody said something awkward in a social setting and it bothered you.

After you choose an event with a negative perception, ask yourself these 2 questions:

- What were your benefits in that situation?
- What would your drawbacks have been in the ideal situation (what you wished had happened)?

Go back and forth with these 2 questions and aim to find at least 25 answers to each of them. Don't stop until you can say wholeheartedly that the situation had *equal* benefits and drawbacks. This is when the exercise is complete.

2. Neutralize a High Charge with Support

Do you have a situation with a very high charge that's taking over your mind? I'm referring to negative charges of 9 or 10 on a scale of 1 to 10—something that no longer allows you to think rationally. Maybe you've been losing business, money, relationships, or health over this issue for a while and it feels impossible to see the other side.

In these situations, the fastest way to get unstuck and avoid suffering for weeks or months is to seek external support. The guidance of an FTP specialist who knows how to ask the right questions and assist you in finding your own answers can be a powerful way to save money, time, and energy. If you want to resolve a problem with a really high charge, reach out to us and we'll connect you with the right specialist who can offer the support you need to overcome the challenge in a matter of hours—not weeks or months.

InspiredLifeCircle.com/book-call-7

CHAPTER 2

THE LAW OF DUALITY IN ACTION

It ain't what you don't know that gets you into trouble. It's what you know for sure that just ain't so.

— anonymous saying, often attributed to Mark Twain

Making the Subconscious Conscious

When we focus on one side of the coin, we naturally miss the other. This is partly due to our biology—the way our eyes are positioned. Our senses are limited to perceiving only what is directly in front of us. Yet our mind can perceive the hidden side, even without our conscious awareness.

What we are aware of is processed and stored in our conscious mind, while what we remain unaware of is stored in our subconscious mind.

In most cases, this dynamic leads us to be conscious of the positives while unaware of the negatives, or vice versa. That's why we may focus on the negatives of a situation while remaining blind to the positives, or we might idealize the positives and ignore the negatives.

The questions you've learned so far, along with the stories shared from real client experiences, are meant to uncover what has been stored in the subconscious mind. Because it's so common for us to interpret situations, events, or relationships as entirely negative, the majority of my work involves asking questions to reveal the benefits, or the positive side, of what appears to be only negative.

Interestingly, I rarely work with individuals who are infatuated with a person or idea because they are typically resistant to breaking that infatuation. When someone falls in love, they don't want to get balanced. Instead, most of the people who come to me want to work on business issues, recurring money patterns, or challenging relationships. In these cases, some of the most useful questions to ask are the first 2 presented in chapter 1: *What are your benefits in this situation, in relation to what's most important to you?* and *What would your drawbacks have been if the opposite had occurred (what you wished had happened)?*

By going back and forth with these questions, you can balance perceptions and bring the hidden aspects of the subconscious into conscious awareness, creating an integrated understanding of the situation and dissolving the charge.

The third question presented in chapter 1 helps dissolve the charge even further and brings the unconscious into the conscious by prompting the client to see that the other person also displayed the opposite: *Where did they do the opposite?* or *In what form do they have the opposite trait?* or *Think of a moment when they did the opposite.*

When No Benefits or Drawbacks Come to Mind

There are 2 circumstances when someone can't find benefits for a perceived negative situation or drawbacks for the ideal situation, and therefore cannot eliminate the charge. The first circumstance is when the charge is so high that one can't find the benefits and drawbacks on their own. It's like a blind spot, so professional support is needed. The second circumstance is when you have an unconscious strategy to keep the story as it is because it is serving you. Let me give you an example.

I had a client, let's call her Samantha, who was determined to work on her relationship with her mother and did most of the work by herself. That's the beauty of the universal laws—once you understand them, you can use them by yourself. You are not dependent on a guru.

Samantha was working on balancing her perceptions when it came to her mother. She had managed to balance most of the charges that were pushing her buttons, but there was one particular instance she simply couldn't resolve: when Samantha was 20, her mother didn't give her money and allow her to travel to another city with her friends. No matter how hard she tried, she couldn't find any benefits in that situation. She found it strange because she had success-fully worked through her mother's other traits on her own.

When she asked me what to do, I told her, "Write down 25 benefits of not finding benefits in this situation. What do you actually gain from not balancing this memory?" She started writing answers, and when she had completed 12 of them she noticed they all began with "I can blame my mother for xyz."

That's when she realized why she didn't genuinely want to balance that memory. In reality, she gained more benefits from holding onto her narrative than from letting it go. It was convenient for her mind to blame her mom and not take any responsibility. The moment she had this realiza-tion, her mind relaxed and she became willing to change her perception. Once this happened, she immediately started finding benefits.

When stakes are high and emotions run so intensely that it becomes impossible to see the situation clearly on your own, it makes sense to seek support. Emotional reactions can lead to significant losses—sometimes tens of thousands or even millions of dollars. That's why my clients have been willing to pay large amounts for one-on-one sessions with me, knowing that it will save them tens of thousands or even millions down the road. In a sense, the service I provide ends up being "free" for them, because the value they gain far outweighs the cost.

Compared to traditional therapeutic methods, what we do is remarkably fast and effective—and the results last a lifetime. Many people prefer working with us over spending years with other therapy methods. Even though the upfront cost may be higher, they solve their challenges much faster, allowing them to move forward with clarity and certainty.

In my view, every therapeutic or coaching method has its place and serves a specific time and context—it's not about right or wrong, but about what is most useful and effective for each individual's unique needs. Our approach simply offers a faster and more effective path for those who resonate with it.

Why "Acceptance" Doesn't Work

A client I met 5 years ago, Mary, had significant conflicts with her mother and was very upset with her. Mary's main issue was that her mother had favored her brother. Her perception was that her mother gave him everything and her nothing. Her mother supported him, saw him as the family genius, and constantly compared her to him. Her brother was the pride of the family, while she felt like nothing in comparison.

Mary left the country and moved far away, across seas and lands, to the United States, where she built a brilliant career.

She wanted to forgive her now elderly mother, to understand and accept her. So she worked with various therapy methods. When we met, she said she was okay with what had happened. She had accepted that "Mom had a tough childhood," and that "she did the best she could at the time."

Mary couldn't have children, which was one of her greatest pains. She lived in an area with access to the most modern medical techniques. Despite this, everything she tried over the years failed. She still couldn't have children and suffered deeply because of it.

Every week she would talk with her husband or friends about her options for achieving conception or whether she should accept the situation and consider adoption.

In my experience, infertility and the relationship with one's mother are connected. I'm not saying it's the only cause, but I have seen many cases where a woman's ability to conceive was linked to how she felt about her mother. Why? If that relationship is strained, why would someone want to repeat what they believe caused them harm? Why bring a child into an experience they perceive as painful?

When Mary joined Power on Heels, our program exclusively for women, she balanced her perceptions regarding her mother. She saw the benefits of what had happened in her relationship with her mother and the drawbacks of the idealized version. She moved past the phase of accepting that "Mom did the best she could" and reached a state of gratitude. The difference between acceptance and gratitude is as vast as the difference between cold leftovers kept in the fridge for 3 weeks and your favorite meal, freshly cooked.

Shortly after Mary balanced her perceptions, she became pregnant and gave birth to a beautiful baby girl.

Some might dismiss it as coincidence, claiming there's no connection between the inner work a person does and their external reality. But in most groups that participated in our Power on Heels program, at least one participant who had struggled with infertility for years became pregnant during the program or shortly after completing it.

Acceptance means you see some benefits of what happened and can say that you understand the situation. That's the reaction at acceptance: "I understand. They did the best they could. I accept that this is how they acted." But the unspoken thoughts connected to the situation remain: *I wish it had been different. It shouldn't have been this way. They should have done things differently, but this was all they could do.*

Besides wishing for a different outcome, another limiting aspect of acceptance is the lingering question in the back of your mind: *Was this really necessary?* You find yourself wondering if there might have been a better way, that perhaps things could have unfolded differently, or that you could have avoided this challenge or suffering altogether.

True balance can't be achieved until you equilibrate the idealized version. The mind continues to hold a charge because it remains attached to that version. Both the nightmare and the fantasy are simultaneously formed in the mind: what happened, which you perceive as negative, and what you wish had happened, which is purely positive without any negatives. Both exist in your mind—one consciously, the other subconsciously. If you don't balance these perceptions, the mind will stay stuck on the idealized version.

The Trap of Smart People

People with a sharper intellect often have the ability to see both sides quickly: the benefits and drawbacks of a situation. On the other hand, those with a narrower perspective or those who hold more rigid, fundamentalist views may struggle to see both sides. Generally speaking, the more educated a person is, the more likely they are to perceive both sides of a situation to varying degrees.

Lawyers are a classic example. They wouldn't be able to do their work well if they didn't have the ability to see both sides—if they held on to a rigid perspective and could not step into the adversary's shoes.

But there's a subtle trap for smart people, which might be important for you to know. Because people with a sharper intellect can identify benefits and drawbacks so quickly, they often stop short of fully working through the situation both quantitatively and qualitatively. They might feel like they've understood it, but in reality they haven't completed the process. As a result, some positive or negative charge remains unresolved—sometimes 20%, sometimes 10%, sometimes only 1%. But the charge is still there.

This lingering imbalance creates a sense of indifference and resignation, where motivation is quite low. People think, "If the benefits and drawbacks are nearly equal, there's no point." But that's exactly the issue: *nearly* equal isn't equal—and that subtle gap breaks the principle of quantitative and qualitative compensation.

Imagine you go to court because someone stole something from you. The judge decides you will be compensated, but the compensation isn't equal to what you lost—neither quantitatively nor qualitatively speaking. Do you think you'll be at peace? Or will you still want to claim what belongs to you? This is exactly what your mind does when the quantitative and qualitative compensation is not fulfilled: it will remain unsettled.

The positive and negative charges can only cancel each other when the benefits equal the drawbacks. Then your outer dynamic will change and you can move on freely.

When the mind is fully balanced, decision-making becomes unnecessary. Instead, you experience complete clarity and you spontaneously act in alignment with what you love. The very need to deliberate over a decision indicates that the mind perceives an imbalance—seeing either more benefits than drawbacks or more drawbacks than benefits in the situation.

When the benefits and drawbacks are *nearly* equal in someone's mind, there are 3 symptoms:

1. Analysis Paralysis

As an example, someone deciding whether to leave a stable job for an entrepreneurial venture might find themselves stuck in an endless loop of pros and cons. The financial security of the current job and the potential freedom of entrepreneurship seem *almost* equally balanced in their mind, causing them to overthink every scenario. This mental tug-of-war keeps them paralyzed, unable to make a choice, and leaves them feeling frustrated and exhausted. Instead of clarity, there is hesitation and overanalysis, which can lead to frustration and a growing aversion to deciding altogether.

2. Postponed Action

Consider someone who has been contemplating joining a fitness program. They recognize the benefits of improved health and confidence but also perceive drawbacks like the cost or time commitment. Because the pros and cons feel *almost* equally weighted, they continually delay signing up, telling themselves they'll decide "next week." As weeks turn into months, the lack of action reinforces their internal struggle, making the decision even harder.

3. Feeling Stuck

Imagine a person who has been thinking about ending a relationship that no longer feels fulfilling. They see the positives of staying—comfort, familiarity, and shared history—*almost* as strongly as they see the negatives—lack of growth, emotional disconnect, and unmet needs. This *almost* balance creates a deep sense of stagnation, as they feel unable to move forward in any direction. Over time, this leads to frustration, self-doubt, and a sense of being trapped in their own life.

Almost balance can lead to a pessimistic view of life where the underlying emotion is futility, and the overarching thought is *Why bother doing anything at all?* When you get up to 99 percent but not 100 percent, it is like coming in second place at some world record—irrelevant. Your mind perceives this feeling of irrelevance and drops the motivation.

I call it "the trap of smart people," because their sharp intellect allows them to quickly identify most of the positives and negatives. Yet this is the reason they often stop short of fully resolving the imbalance—reaching 90 percent, 95 percent, or even 99 percent—leaving them caught in the struggle of making a decision.

The key is to recognize this pattern and go all the way in neutralizing a charge, ensuring that the charge is fully resolved and freeing the mind for inspired, spontaneous action.

2 Other Mistakes People Make about the Law of Duality

In the previous section, we explored a common mistake people make in applying the law of duality: reaching a state of acceptance and indifference by not fully balancing the perception. In this section, you will see 2 other common mistakes or misunderstandings.

1. Confusing Balancing Perceptions with Simple Reframing

When people with some experience in personal development learn about the law of duality, they often think, "Oh, that's reframing." My answer is, "No it's not," and here's why.

In neuro-linguistic programming (NLP), reframing is the process of changing the way a person perceives a situation, behavior, or experience by altering its meaning or context—without changing the facts. The goal is to shift the emotional or psychological response to something more resourceful or empowering. An example could be, "failure doesn't mean you're incapable—it means you're learning what doesn't work," or "being stubborn may seem negative, but in a crisis, that same trait becomes determination."

This is the equivalent of looking at one side of the coin, and reframing is flipping the coin and saying, "it's not heads, it's tails." Balancing perception is seeing the *whole* coin—both sides at the same time. That's a big difference.

The second difference is that reframing doesn't seek the perfection of the situation—it's simply changing the angle and turning the situation in your favor. But seeing the perfection of life is what makes the mind stronger. That perfection lies in the integration of complementary opposites: support and challenge.

The third difference is that reframing often doesn't follow the principle of quantitative and qualitative compensation. When that's the case, it may be effective in the moment, but won't resolve the problem long-term. That said, I'm not denying the usefulness of reframing—I'm simply clarifying the difference between reframing and applying the law of duality.

2. Assuming the Goal Is to Turn Negative into Positive.

Expressions often used in the personal development world, like "turning challenges into blessings," may confuse people. The goal of balancing perceptions is to see both sides equally. When one truly sees that there are as many drawbacks as benefits to a situation, they've completed the process. It's not about turning something bad into some-thing good—it's about seeing that it is neither good nor bad. This is when the mind becomes free and moves to a higher level of awareness.

The 4 Opiates of the Masses

If you're a parent, you've likely set the goal to stay calm no matter what, at least once in your life. This decision often follows moments when you've lost your temper with your children. Maybe it wasn't even their fault—maybe you had a bad day or an emotionally overwhelming one, and you lashed out. Then you promised yourself you wouldn't do it again. You might have woken up in the morning and said to yourself, "Alright, today I'll be calm, loving, and patient with the kids. I'll gently respond to their needs. If they throw a tantrum, I'll lovingly take them in my arms rather than react." And in your mind, you plan to use all the techniques you intuitively understand for managing your child's behavior.

But what happens is that the more determined you are in the morning to stay calm throughout the day, the easier it becomes to lose your temper. When the kids wake up and something happens—like spilling a glass of milk or getting jam on their shirt right before leaving the house—you lose it. The stronger your intention to stay calm, the easier it is to erupt—and afterward, you feel even worse for losing your temper.

The struggle to stay calm shows a deeper truth: the harder we push for one side—like peace or happiness—the more its opposite seems to surface. This reflects the law of duality, which reminds us that every coin has 2 sides—in both our personal lives and the world around us.

There are 4 major spheres of our lives where the law of duality is often overlooked. In these areas, people strive for one side of the equation while trying to get rid of the other, resulting in frustration and futility.

The first one is psychology, where people seek happiness while trying to get rid of sadness. The second is sociology, where people seek peace while attempting to eliminate conflict. The third is medicine, where people seek health while striving to escape disease. And the fourth is religion, where people seek heaven while trying to avoid hell.

The law of duality is woven into the very fabric of our reality, evident in every branch of science and every aspect of life. How, then, can we believe it's possible to have one side without the other? How can we imagine a life where someone is always happy and never sad? A world with only peace and no conflict? Perfect health without the natural cycles of illness and recovery—especially when the number of cells being born in a healthy adult body equals the number of cells dying every day? How can we envision eternal bliss in heaven, where only the positives exist and no negatives?

I call this wishful thinking the 4 "opiates of the masses."[12] The more educated and aware people become, the more they recognize that there are 2 sides to every coin. No matter how much we wish it were different, it's impossible to have one side without the other.

Conversely, the less educated or less aware people are, the more gullible they are, and thus more vulnerable to scams and false promises. This lack of understanding makes them easy targets for those who exploit their desire for a one-sided reality, perpetuating illusions that lead to disappointment and manipulation. One classic example of this is the "get rich quick" schemes, which present an idealized version of success without effort. Because people aren't trained to question the full picture, they often buy into the fantasy—and pay the price when reality hits. Many people lose their savings or fall into debt this way.

There is, however, a hidden order here. It shows itself when pain becomes a teacher—pushing people to see beyond the surface. The hurt caused by manipulation or disappointment often breaks the illusions that were once believed, helping people who are less aware to see both sides of the equation. They learn through this, grow stronger, and become more aware. What feels like a setback turns into a step forward—

12 Expression coined by Karl Marx.

helping them move from being naive to becoming wiser and more confident.

The 4 Types of Feedback

My dear friend and client, Dr. Kim Jobst, former editor in chief of the *The Journal of Integrative Medicine*, published a paper in 1999 called "The Diseases of Meaning."

According to Dr. Jobst, many times disease is not something to get rid of, but a sign that the body and mind are trying to stay balanced. Instead of seeing illness as a problem, he believes it can be a message that something needs to change, whether it be certain relationships, the environment, or thinking patterns. One of his favorite sayings is, "pain points the finger to the unlearned lesson."

Picture someone going to a party. The evening starts with seafood paella and a crisp white wine, but soon derails into barbecue ribs with mac and cheese, chased by a bitter beer. As the night spirals, greasy pepperoni and anchovy pizza collides with espresso martinis, the flavors waging war. The final blow: fiery Thai green curry drowned in spiced rum, the creamy coconut and bitter alcohol sealing their fate. By night's end, the party-goer's stomach is a battlefield, guaranteeing a next-day disaster of nausea, heartburn, and regret.

The discomfort they'll feel the next morning isn't an illness— it's healthy feedback. They could go to a doctor, hide the details of their night, and get painkillers to silence the symptoms. But the symptoms aren't the problem. They're the body's way of guiding us back to balance.

When we don't see both sides of an event, we receive 4 types of feedback, each happening in stages. First comes physiological feedback—we feel it in our body. If we ignore it, we often experience psychological feedback. If that goes unnoticed, we get sociological feedback, and finally, theological feedback.[13] Let's take a look at them, one by one.

Physiological feedback occurs when your body sends you signals, from butterflies in your stomach to acute pains. *Psychological* feedback is your intuition trying to get you back to center. It whispers things like "it's too good to be true" or "there's got to be a silver lining." *Sociological* feedback happens when other people help you become balanced by showing you the other side. When we ignore our body, our intuition, and the people around us, we invite Murphy's Law—the popular name for *theological* feedback—and unexplained events unfold.[14]

Let me give you an example for each of the 4 types of feedback, starting with *physiological*. Many years ago, I was at home, suffering from a terrible headache, and a gallbladder crisis was also brewing. The pain gripped one side of my head, the light felt unbearable, and all I could do was stay in my room doing nothing because I was exhausted from the migraine. I couldn't move, and kept trying to find a position where the pain eased just enough for me to breathe.

---

13 I first encountered these 4 types of feedback in the work of Dr. John Demartini.

14 Murphy's Law is a humorous proverb expressing how things often don't go as planned, especially in complex situations. It captures the feeling that problems seem to show up exactly when you least expect or want them to, as if there's some invisible rule that makes the worst-case scenario oddly likely—without any logical explanation.

I had just learned that headaches often signify an inner conflict between what you truly want and what you believe others expect from you. So I lay in my bed, trying to identify the inner conflict I was experiencing.

I noticed that the conflict was between what I wanted and what I thought my mother wanted from me. In other words, a conflict between what was truly important to me versus what was pleasing to my mother. As soon as I pinpointed the issue, my headache almost vanished. I'd never been able to stop a headache like that before. It was the first time I truly saw how quickly the mind can influence the body.

Now let's see an example of how *psychological* feedback works. Nearly twenty years ago, when I was running Transylvania's leading recruitment agency, a man who appeared to be the perfect client walked through our doors. He was polished, confident, and had an ambitious request: he wanted us to fill 12 positions, from top management to an entire sales team.

I felt excitement—12 recruitment projects from a single client was not common at all. But as I listened to him, my intuition whispered that something seemed too good to be true.

After detailing his requirements, he said, "Prepare the contracts. Let's sign them and get started." I nodded but turned to my team afterward and said, "We'll begin the search when the money is in our account."

Days passed, and despite signing the contracts, he hadn't made any payments, so I decided to dig deeper. I searched his name online and found an article that confirmed my intuition. He had a history of making grand promises but failing to deliver. Companies had suffered significant losses because of his unreliability.

I sat back and exhaled, realizing how close we had come to disaster. If we had jumped into these projects without securing payment, my small team would have spent months working for nothing—causing serious financial damage to our business.

The purpose of intuition is to guide us back to center—it's a feedback mechanism. Many people confuse intuition with instinct or impulse. Instinct helps us avoid danger, much like animals avoiding predators. Impulse draws us toward something, similar to how animals are attracted to prey. While instinct and impulse are responses shared by mammals, intuition is uniquely human. Next time you feel your intuition speaking to you, don't mistake it for instinct.

When we ignore the first and second feedback mechanisms—physiological and psychological—the external world provides *sociological* feedback. People around us, whether close or distant, will point out what we fail to see. This is sociological feedback.

A few years ago, a well-known influencer sought me out because she had been harshly criticized publicly and her confidence was shaken. Before the controversial report aired, her colleagues warned her multiple times to stop posting outrageous pictures of what she was doing. They told her to stop flaunting the handbags she was buying and to tone down her lifestyle displays because it looked like she was showing off.

Of course, she also got plenty of criticism on social media, but she ignored it. Her colleagues warned her again, "Hey,

THE LAW OF DUALITY IN ACTION

be careful, stop doing this." But she brushed them off once again.

In the end, a TV report about her aired, followed by 2 harsh articles that deeply humbled her. It's rare for someone to face public criticism without having first come across as arrogant or cocky. Public criticism is a form of feedback, helping steer us back toward balance.

Finally, *theological* feedback arrives when we ignore every other form of feedback—when we don't listen to our body symptoms, when we don't listen to our intuition, and we refuse to listen to others.

Years ago, when my daughter was still in school, I found myself drawn to a new group of friends. I was captivated by them, convinced they were extraordinary, that they had something I lacked. When they planned a beach trip I was determined to go, no matter what.

But everything pointed to no. I had no one to watch my daughter. I had an important work project. There were logistical issues at every turn. My body signaled unease— tension and stomachache. My intuition whispered against it. Even my best friend, seeing what I refused to see, told me these people weren't who I imagined them to be.

I ignored it all. I rearranged plans, forced solutions, and did whatever it took to make the trip happen. Then something happened that I couldn't ignore.

Just outside the city, I realized I had forgotten something at home and wanted to check my bags. I pulled over and opened the car door slightly—then hesitated. A convoy of trucks was approaching fast.

The first truck passed, sending a violent gust of air that yanked the door wide open. The second truck came an instant later—and ripped the door completely off. I sat there, staring at the empty space where my car door had been, and I understood the message: stop going on this holiday. In the following days, I realized that the people I had put on a pedestal were not who I believed they were, and my infatuation began to fade.

These 4 types of feedback are life's gift, constantly guiding us to see the "other side" that we are unconscious of, and to get back to center. Learn to use them effectively and in your favor. Listen to your intuition and your body first, so the feedback doesn't escalate to a social level—or worse, to Murphy's level.

The Law of Duality in the Realm of Healing

The link between mind and body is profound, and science is only beginning to uncover its depth. The connection between our thoughts and physical health is real, but still largely a mystery. Over the past few years, I've witnessed remarkable physical healing in people's lives. Jose is one of them.

I met Jose, a 78-year-old gentleman, during one of my webinars in early 2025. His story moved me—and many others—to tears. Here's how I remember and wish to honor his story, which he shared in one of our online meetings:

Hello everyone, I'm Jose.

Yesterday was a very special day for me after Monica's presentation.

I sat quietly for a while and asked myself a question I had never truly dared to ask before: What was good about my mother dying when I was not even 2 years old?

It felt almost impossible to find an answer. I don't have memories of her—only a deep sense that I was shy, afraid, and abandoned. My father, struggling with his own nerves and pain, frightened me. When he came home, I used to hide under the bed.

That was my world—until one day, a woman came into our lives. She was my father's first love from his studies in Germany. She stepped in and cared for me and my sisters. She raised us. She gave me protection. And now, looking back, I realize—she changed my life entirely.

Yesterday, at 78 years old, I had a realization I never had before. I always thought something was missing in me. That I lacked an anchor. That I wasn't fully prepared for the world. Even though I built a life—studied in Germany, earned degrees, built relationships, and returned to Bolivia—there was always this quiet sense of not being whole.

But yesterday, something shifted. It hit me: maybe the "bad" thing I held on to—my mother's death—also brought something profoundly good into my life. It forced me to grow in another way. It led me to discover protection in a completely unexpected form.

And with that realization, I felt something lift.

I've been struggling with a lung disease for over 15 years. Doctors have told me there's nothing I can do. That the lungs don't regenerate. That this is the one organ that doesn't heal. I've tried everything, hoping to breathe normally again.

But yesterday, after seeing things differently, I began to sing— loudly. For the first time in years, I felt joy. I could breathe freely—without cortisone, without medicine. I don't know if the illness is gone, but I feel alive. I feel happy.

Thank you, Monica. Your work opened a window in me that had never been opened before. Thank you from the bottom of my heart.

Jose's story is one of many I've been privileged to witness—from pregnancies once thought impossible, to cancer remissions—all connected with balancing judgments through the law of duality.

Without the Pair of Opposites You Get Stuck in Moral Paradoxes

"It ain't what you don't know that gets you into trouble. It's what you know for sure that just ain't so." This statement, often attributed to Mark Twain, reminds me how little we truly know about the fundamental questions of life.

My husband grew up in a family deeply rooted in Christian traditions. His father is a priest, his grandfather was a priest, and several uncles are also priests. This legacy of faith shaped much of his childhood, while also sparking a curious and inquisitive mind. One particular memory stands out to him—a moment that occurred when he was about 10 years old and wrestling with profound questions about the nature of God and the existence of evil.

One evening he turned to his father and asked, "Dad, is it true that God is everywhere, knows everything, and can do anything?"

His father, in his calm and authoritative way, affirmed, "Yes, according to our faith and scriptures, God is omnipotent, omnipresent, and omniscient."

The boy's brow furrowed as he processed this. "Then why does God allow the devil to do bad things? If God is everywhere and sees everything, doesn't that make Him responsible for what the devil does? If I'm with another kid and he steals something, people would say I'm guilty too because I didn't stop him. Doesn't that mean God is an accomplice to the devil?"

The question was piercing, and his father paused before responding. Finally, he said, "God allows the devil to tempt man so that man can exercise free will. It's a test of faith and choice."

But this answer didn't sit well with the 10-year-old. He pushed further. "If God created Adam and Eve, and put them in the Garden of Eden, and told them not to eat from the tree, didn't He already know what was going to happen? He's omniscient, right? So didn't He set them up to fail?"

The room fell silent. His father's explanation about free will seemed insufficient to a boy grappling with the paradoxes of faith.

Years later, my husband and I reflected on this conversation together. When he was 10 years old, he unknowingly stumbled onto a philosophical conundrum known as the Epicurean paradox, formulated by the ancient Greek philosopher Epicurus (341 - 270 BCE). It's a 4-sentence argument questioning the coexistence of an all-powerful, all-knowing, and benevolent God with the reality of evil.

1. If God is willing to prevent evil but not able, then He is not omnipotent.

2. If God is able to prevent evil but not willing, then He is malevolent.

3. If God is both willing and able, then why does evil exist?

4. If God is neither willing nor able, then why call Him God?

This philosophical riddle has challenged theologians and thinkers for centuries, giving rise to theodicies—attempts to reconcile God's goodness with the existence of evil. None of them can offer a definitive answer.

When you try to separate the pair of opposites, you inevitably encounter moral paradoxes like this—paradoxes so straightforward that even a 10-year-old could recognize them without ever having studied the philosophers.

But for my husband at age 10, the paradox was not a philosophical exercise. It was deeply personal. He didn't stop there. Another day he asked his father, "Could a 1-year-old ever make you truly upset?"

"No," his father replied, smiling. "A 1-year-old is too young to do anything that would really upset me."

"How old are you, Dad?"

"I'm 38," his father said.

"So there's a 37-year difference between you and a 1-year-old?"

"That's right."

The boy's next question stopped his father in his tracks. "What's the difference between you and God? Isn't it way more than 37 years? If a 1-year-old can't upset you, how could humans ever think they could upset God?"

This childlike yet profound reasoning may offer a different perspective for our understanding of God. Maybe the gap between us and God is greater than the gap between ants and humans. What if our understanding of God is even more limited than an ant's understanding of humans? Isn't it arrogant to claim we understand God's nature and intentions? Most people would admit they know nothing about ants,[15] yet some of us speak with conviction about God. How strange is that?

This perspective also explains why I've deliberately chosen to reference very few texts from the Bible in this book—because it's more complex. We'll have a separate book on how the universal laws are reflected in the Bible, and maybe other religious writings too. Many Christians believe that God is only positive and the devil is only negative, but even the scriptures challenge this oversimplification. Isaiah 45:7 reads, "I form the light, and create darkness: I make peace, and create evil: I the Lord do all these things."[16]

---

15 Ants are extraordinary creatures who have existed for over 100 million years. They can form massive super-colonies spanning thousands of kilometers and lift 50 times their body weight. They have 2 stomachs—one for digesting food and one for sharing it. They communicate using chemical pheromones and "farm" other insects, like aphids, for honeydew. Known for their division of labor, some ants are also excellent architects—some build nests with ventilation systems, while others create rafts to survive floods. Found on every continent except Antarctica, ants are one of the most successful and adaptable creatures on earth.

16 King James Version (KJV).

Maybe a wiser approach would be to study God's work through the natural laws of the universe, as great minds like Thomas Aquinas, Giordano Bruno, Galileo Galilei, and Nicolaus Copernicus did.

Strength and Weakness of the Mind

When we want to weaken a structure, we take it apart and break it into pieces. This approach makes the problem easier to tackle. A mechanic, for example, disassembles an engine to gain control over its parts—because as a whole, the engine is too complex to work with directly.

The ancients understood this principle well. Caesar famously said "*divide et impera*," which means "divide and rule," or "divide and conquer." This strategy of division has been applied many times throughout history to weaken and control the population.

Today, almost every financial guru will advise you to destroy your credit card unless you have strong financial discipline. Credit cards are one of the most effective tools for weakening financial stability because they separate pain from pleasure. You experience the pleasure of buying now and face the pain of paying next month. With too much space and time separating the 2, the brain fails to connect pain and pleasure, leaving people vulnerable to poor financial decisions.

This principle applies to the mind as well. When we separate the pairs of opposites—pain and pleasure, good and bad, benefits and drawbacks—our mind becomes weaker. But when we integrate these opposites, our mind becomes stronger. Separation weakens the mind. Integration empowers the mind.

Empedocles (494-434 BCE), the ancient Greek philosopher, said that elements are combined and separated by 2 opposing forces: love and strife.[17] Love brings elements together, creating unity and harmony, while strife separates them, leading to division and chaos.

Throughout history, people have understood that unity is synonymous with power and division means weakness. That's why they created powerful structures like the European Union, United States of America, United Kingdom, and United Arab Emirates.

Thinking in Opposites Means Better Problem-Solving

In 2019, a team of Italian researchers led by Erika Branchini at the University of Verona, along with colleagues from the University of Macerata, set out to solve a persistent mystery in cognitive psychology: Why are some problems so hard to solve, until suddenly they're not?[18]

These "difficult problems" often lead to those famous "aha moments," but scientists didn't fully understand how people reached these breakthroughs. Previous research suggested that thinking about opposites, like inside-outside or large-small, might help—but nobody knew the best way to use this strategy.

---

17 Empedocles, "Fragments of Empedocles," trans. John Burnet, in *Early Greek Philosophy*, 3rd ed. (Adam & Charles Black, 1920), chap. 5, https://en.wikisource.org/wiki/Fragments_of_Empedocles.

18 Ivana Bianchi et al., "Overtly Prompting People to 'Think in Opposites' Supports Insight Problem Solving," *Thinking & Reasoning* 26, no. 1 (2019): 31–67, https://doi.org/10.1080/13546783.2018.1553738.

The researchers gathered 240 undergraduate students and divided them into 3 groups. The first group received training in how to think about opposites. The second group was told to write down pairs of opposites, and the third group was asked to simply think about opposites. Each category had 7-and-a-half minutes to solve 6 different spatial puzzles.

As the results came in, a clear pattern emerged. The first group, which received proper training, significantly out-performed the second group by about 45%. The second group, which wrote down opposites, did about 31% better than the third group, which just thought about them. So the group that had a systematic approach to the pairs of oppo-sites succeeded in solving about 76% of the given problems compared to those who only thought about the opposites.

If the study had compared the success rate to a group that hadn't focused on the pair of opposites at all, the results would likely have been significantly higher—maybe close to 100%.

The findings were published in *Psychological Applications and Trends 2019*, contributing to our understanding of how the human mind can benefit by integrating pairs of opposites, and the effectiveness of integration vs. separation.

How the Mind Gets Weaker or Stronger

In my observation, the strength of the mind exists on a continuum, and is determined by the individual's capacity to see both sides of a situation and how well they can hold the pair of opposites in their mind. In his book *Beyond Good and Evil*, Friedrich Nietzsche remarked, "The strength of a person's spirit would then be measured by how much 'truth' he could tolerate."[19]

When an individual starts to separate pain from pleasure, good from bad, and benefits from drawbacks, they embark on a path that weakens the mind. The next stage of this separation involves disconnecting cause and effect. As illustrated in the example of credit card usage, when people fail to connect pain and pleasure or benefits and drawbacks, they similarly fail to connect cause and effect. This disconnection leads to dissociation, where individuals no longer perceive themselves as agents in their own lives. They begin to believe that control over their life lies with external forces—their boss, politicians, religious institutions—but not themselves. In this state, blame is also attributed to others but not to oneself.

As this process continues, the mind deteriorates further, descending into paranoia. Paranoia manifests as a belief that others intend harm, interpreting neutral events as threats, and feeling constantly watched or followed. Left unchecked, this degradation can progress to schizophrenia and disintegration of mental coherence. The term *schizophrenia* originates from the Greek words *skhizein* (to split) and *phrēn* (mind), signifying a complete split of the mind.[20]

---

19 Friedrich Nietzsche, *Beyond Good and Evil: Prelude to a Philosophy of the Future*, trans. Judith Norman (Cambridge University Press, 2002), Section 39.

20 This explanation highlights why I believe psychedelics can be particularly dangerous for individuals with strong moral beliefs who see the world in rigid terms of right and wrong. Psychiatrists refer to psychedelics as "non-specific amplifiers of awareness," meaning they intensify whatever is already present in the mind. For someone who is already highly polarized in their thinking, a psychedelic experience could amplify that polarization to the point of mental instability, potentially leading to a permanent psychological breakdown. Even the most open-minded psychiatrists, including those who support the use of psychedelics in some cases, strongly caution

Conversely, on the other end of the spectrum, when an individual integrates the pairs of opposites day by day, they gain increasing agency over their life. They recognize themselves as the creators of their experiences and as the ones in charge of their destiny. This perspective cultivates a sense of control and self-mastery, culminating in a state known as *pronoia*. *Pronoia* is seeing things *on* the way, not *in* the way, perceiving events as happening *for* them, rather than *against* them. In this state, individuals align with the flow of life's energy, enabling them to achieve ever greater things.

Thus, the path to mental strength lies in the integration of opposites, which leads to a state of certainty, gratitude and love. This then translates into more profound achievements, self-mastery, and an inspired life.

Integration of Opposites Is an Ever-Evolving Journey

One might think that integrating opposites leads to a state of eternal peace or enlightenment, where nothing can bother you anymore. As you will discover throughout the pages of this book, however, integrating opposites is an ever-evolving journey of empowering the mind.

Consider this: when you are 10 years old, unexpectedly receiving $10 might make your entire day. On the other hand, losing $10 could feel devastating. This isn't really about the money itself. Replace the $10 with a toy, an ice

---

against their use for anyone with even mild mental health challenges. Some of my clients have shared that working one-on-one with me felt like a psychedelic experience—without any substances. By balancing the mind with the right questions, they reached a state of pure love and gratitude, surpassing even what they had experienced with magic mushrooms or ayahuasca.

cream, or any problem proportionate to that amount—the principle is what matters.

Now imagine being 20 years old. At this stage, unexpectedly receiving $100 could make your day, while a $100 fine might ruin it. At age 30, the threshold grows: a surprise of $1000 is thrilling, but a fine of the same amount could feel overwhelming. By age 40, a windfall of $10,000 could bring joy, while a loss of $10,000 could cause significant stress. This progression could go on and on.

But if you are 40 years old and I give $10 to you or take $10 from you, it likely wouldn't affect you at all. Why? Because you have mastered that level of opposites. You've integrated the giving and taking at that scale. The $10 symbolize a pair of opposites—giving and taking—and your ability to transcend them at this level reflects mental growth.

The greater the pairs of opposites you can integrate, the more stable and stronger your mind becomes. Think about it: you probably know people for whom a $10 problem is a massive challenge, while others can manage million-dollar issues multiple times a day. The difference lies in their capacity to hold and reconcile complementary opposites in their mind at any given moment.

Some individuals, for example, can handle being despised by half the world while having the admiration of the other half. In contrast, others might lose sleep over a minor disagreement with a neighbor. This book will guide you in strengthening your mind, supporting you to integrate increasingly complex pairs of opposites on your path to self-mastery.

Practical Application

Here are 2 practical actions to use this information and increase its impact in your life.

1. Experience What "Beyond Acceptance" Feels Like, on Your Own

Take someone else's action that you've already "accepted" in your life, but deep down you still wish had been different. I suggest you choose something with a mild charge for practice (intensity of 4 or 5 on a scale from 1 to 10). Here are a few examples for your inspiration:

- Your mom criticised you.
- Your boss fired you.
- You received a medical diagnosis.
- Your friend chose somebody else over you.
- Your child behaved rudely at an event.
- A team member made a mistake and you missed a deadline.
- A client did not pay you on time.
- Your partner did not support your education.
- The nanny didn't show up, so you missed a social event.
- Your boss chose someone else for the team or role you wanted.

After you choose an event, ask yourself these 2 questions:

- What were your benefits in that situation?

- What would your drawbacks have been in the ideal situation—what you wish had happened?

Write at least 25 answers for each of them. Don't stop until you can say wholeheartedly that the situation has *equal* benefits and drawbacks.

Be specific, not general—otherwise your mind will not believe the answers. What were you able to do or not do as a result of each benefit or drawback?

When you have at least 50 answers, ask yourself the "verification questions":

- Do I perceive I had equal benefits and drawbacks from their action?
- Do I perceive that the ideal situation (what I wished had happened) would have had equal drawbacks and benefits?
- Am I grateful for their action as it was, and can I feel the perfection within it?

If the benefits and drawbacks are not perceived as being equal, and if you don't see its perfection—meaning, you still want to change it—please write more benefits and drawbacks until you reach a state of love and gratitude for what has happened and there is no desire to change it. This is when the exercise is complete.

2. Reduce the Time and Effort Spent on Decision-Making, with Support

There's a moment—often around 4 pm—when even "simple" choices feel like emotional weightlifting. Coffee or tea? Reply or postpone? You're not lazy. You're depleted. Not because the day was hard, but because every small decision chipped away at your clarity.

It's not the "big" decisions that drain you. It's the accumulation of 37 small ones before 10 am—each pulling you further from presence. The worst part? You stop hearing your own intuition. You outsource decisions to urgency. Or worse, to autopilot.

True freedom comes when you allow yourself to go all the way, achieving perfect balance that leads to spontaneous and inspired action. If you often find yourself wrestling with difficult decisions—especially around business or money—and investing significant time and energy in weighing every pro and con, know that there's a more aligned and efficient way.

We can connect you with an FTP specialist who can support you in identifying the root cause of the difficulty around decision-making—and guide you in transforming the underlying pattern. Apply for a free session at:

InspiredLifeCircle.com/book-call-7

CHAPTER 3

THE LAW OF DUALITY IN HISTORY AND SCIENCE

*Everything is dual; everything has poles; everything
has its pair of opposites; like and unlike are the
same; opposites are identical in nature, but different
in degree; extremes meet.*

— *The Kybalion*, The Three Initiates

If history or science are not your favorite subject, feel free to breeze through this chapter and jump ahead to the next one. For those of you who appreciate some background context, I'm confident this section will be a delight.

How People Discovered the Law of Duality

A dear friend told me that the concept of universal laws sounds a bit too "woo-woo" for him. And perhaps that's true for many modern men and women who rely on concrete, tangible ideas to navigate life. For centuries, biased interpretations were often imposed by various religious leaders, making skepticism a natural response in today's world, where science is the dominant lens through which we understand reality. To offer clarity for those who feel this way, in this chapter I'd like to provide a deeper context about the law of duality.

Let's explore its origins—how the law of duality was discovered, how it has emerged and evolved over the past 5000 years, and who wrote about it. Then we will take a look at what modern science says. This chapter is not an exhaustive account, but rather a collection of key reference points to help you understand the law of duality's evolution and context throughout history.

Ancient Egypt

In ancient Egyptian writings from c. 3000–500 BCE, the concept of complementary opposites was central to their worldview, cosmology, and religion. These opposites were seen as interconnected and interdependent, working together to sustain balance and order in the universe.

Pyramid Texts (c. 2400–2300 BCE) and Coffin Texts (c. 2100–1800 BCE)

These texts describe the struggle between Ma'at and Isfet as a cosmic and eternal dynamic that maintained the balance of the universe. Ma'at represented truth, justice, harmony, and cosmic order. Ma'at was personified as a goddess and symbolized the ideal state of the world. Isfet represented chaos, disorder, and injustice. The concept of Isfet was not personified to the same extent as Ma'at but was seen as the opposite force to be controlled. The pharaoh's role was to uphold Ma'at by ensuring justice, stability, and proper rituals to prevent the intrusion of Isfet.

Other dualities known in ancient Egypt, such as Geb (earth) and Nut (sky) or Osiris (life) and Seth (death), embodied complementary opposites necessary for creation and renewal.

Hermeticism

The profound ideas in the ancient writings of Egypt were distilled and refined in Hermeticism, a body of esoteric thought that emerged in the first few centuries of the Common Era. Hermeticism served as a bridge, preserving and evolving the wisdom of ancient Egypt into a form that influenced later Western mystical and philosophical traditions.

Corpus Hermeticum, written in Greek during the early Roman Empire (c. 2nd–3rd century CE), often speaks of the unity underlying duality. For example, the divine essence (the "All") encompasses both masculine and feminine principles, which together generate creation. These principles are often referred to as Logos (active, masculine) and Sophia (receptive, feminine). The universe is a product of balance and harmony between opposing forces, like chaos and order or motion and stillness, reflecting the overarching unity of the divine.

Hermetic texts describe the principle of polarity in *The Kybalion*, which asserts "everything is dual; everything has poles; everything has its pair of opposites; like and unlike are the same; opposites are identical in nature, but different in degree; extremes meet."[21] This principle reflects the idea that opposites, such as hot and cold or light and dark, are not fundamentally different but rather degrees of the same phenomenon. The interplay of opposites is seen as essential for creation and transformation.

Ancient Babylon

The ancient Babylonians were advanced astronomers and saw duality in celestial cycles. In the cycle of day and night, controlled by the sun god Shamash and the moon god Sin, their interplay symbolized the rhythm of life. The seasonal cycles of planting and harvest, and myths like Ishtar's descent into the underworld, reflect the interplay between growth and decay, life and death.

The Goddess Ishtar (Inanna)

Worshiped back in the Uruk period in ancient Sumer (c. 4000–3100 BCE), she was the goddess of both love and war, at the same time. Ishtar embodies the duality of creation and destruction, nurturing and conflict.

Code of Hammurabi (c. 1750 BCE)

One of the earliest written set of laws, the Code of Hammurabi reflects duality in human governance. The Babylonians viewed justice as a balance between opposing claims or forces, such as punishment and restoration, or fairness and

---

21 Three Initiates, *The Kybalion: A Study of the Hermetic Philosophy of Ancient Egypt and Greece* (Yogi Publication Society, 1908), 10.

retribution. The king was a mediator between divine will (cosmic order) and human society (potential chaos).

Architecture

The Babylonians had impressive buildings called ziggurats, such as the famous Etemenanki (possibly associated with the Tower of Babel). These ziggurats symbolized the connection between heaven (the divine) and earth (the human). They were physical embodiments of bridging opposites, uniting the spiritual and material realms.

In ancient Babylon, complementary opposites like chaos and order, light and dark, life and death, and male and female were fundamental to their understanding of creation and existence. These opposites were not antagonistic but interdependent, with their interaction driving the cycles of life and maintaining cosmic balance. This perspective laid the groundwork for later philosophical and religious systems that also explored the interplay of dualities.

Ancient India

In ancient Indian writings, the concept of complementary opposites is deeply rooted in metaphysical, cosmological, and spiritual thought. These opposites are often seen as interdependent, dynamic forces essential to the functioning of the cosmos, human existence, and spiritual realization. They appear prominently in Vedic texts, Upanishads, Samkhya philosophy, Tantra, and Buddhist writings. Here are some examples.

Vedic Texts (c. 1500–500 BCE)

Particularly in the *Rigveda*, dualities are presented as complementary aspects of creation. For example, the "Purusha

Sukta" describes the cosmic being, Purusha, as the source of the universe. Complementing Purusha is the material aspect of existence, later identified as Prakriti. These dual principles are the foundation of creation: Purusha (consciousness) represents the unchanging, eternal aspect, while Prakriti (nature) embodies dynamism, diversity, and transformation.

Upanishad (c. 800–200 BCE)

This Hindu religious text emphasizes the duality of Brahman (the ultimate reality) and Maya (illusion or the manifested world). Brahman is the infinite, formless essence underlying all existence. Maya is the appearance of dualities, diversity, and multiplicity in the material world, which veils the unity of Brahman. Liberation (Moksha) involves transcending the perception of dualities to realize unity.

Bhagavad Gita (c. 5th–2nd century BCE)

Lord Krishna advises the warrior Arjuna to overcome his moral dilemmas and to rise above dualities like pleasure and pain, gain and loss, and success and failure, achieving equanimity and self-realization.

Tantric Traditions (c. 500 CE onwards)

Duality is embodied in Shiva (pure consciousness, masculine) and Shakti (creative energy, feminine). Shiva is inactive without Shakti, and Shakti cannot exist without Shiva. Their union symbolizes the dynamic balance of opposites necessary for creation and spiritual awakening. This duality is expressed through the kundalini energy: the ascent of Shakti through the chakras to merge with Shiva at the crown of the head (sahasrara), representing enlightenment.

Ancient China

Ancient Chinese texts explored the idea of complementary opposites as essential to understanding cosmology, philosophy, and everyday life. Rather than opposing each other, these forces were seen as interdependent and transformative. This theme runs through Taoist, Confucian, and cosmological writings.

I Ching (Book of Changes)

Written as early as 1000 BCE, describes the interplay of yin and yang as the basis of cosmic change. Hexagrams in the *I Ching* represent different configurations of yin and yang energies.

The concept of yin and yang is perhaps the most well-known representation of complementary opposites in Chinese philosophy. Yin represents qualities such as darkness, femininity, passivity, coldness, and receptivity. Yang represents qualities such as light, masculinity, activity, heat, and assertiveness. The dynamic balance between yin and yang governs the natural order of the universe. They are not fixed, but constantly transform into each other—as symbolized by the taijitu, or yin-yang symbol.

Tao-Te Ching (c. 6th century BCE, attributed to Laozi)

This Chinese philosophical literature describes the Tao (the Way) as the source of all dualities, emphasizing that opposites are necessary for harmony: "Under heaven, all can see beauty as beauty only because there is ugliness. All can know good as good only because there is evil."[22]

---

22 Laozi, *Tao Te Ching*, trans. D.C. Lau (Penguin Books, 1963), ch. 2.

Zhuangzi (c. 4th century BCE)

This ancient Chinese text expands on Laozi's ideas, discussing how apparent opposites are interconnected and transform into each other, challenging rigid categorizations.

Traditional Chinese Medicine

TCM is based on the yin-yang theory and the balance of qi. Disease arises when there is an imbalance between yin and yang. Yin disorders, such as the common cold, or fatigue, are treated with yang-enhancing therapies like heat or activity. Yang disorders, such as fever, or hyperactivity, are treated with yin-enhancing therapies like cooling and rest.

Ancient Greece

In ancient Greek writings, complementary opposites like light and dark, order and chaos, soul and body, love and strife are foundational to understanding the universe, human nature, and moral life. Greek thinkers often sought to reconcile or transcend these opposites, emphasizing their interdependence and the harmony they create. This exploration of dualities profoundly influenced Western philosophy, shaping metaphysical and ethical thought for centuries.

Heraclitus (c. 535–475 BCE)

Heraclitus is the earliest Greek philosopher to explicitly discuss the unity of opposites. Heraclitus had significant influence on Plato, Aristotle, and the Stoics, among many others. Hegel (1770–1831) famously stated, "There is no proposition of Heraclitus which I have not adopted in my logic."[23] Nietzsche's work was influenced by Heraclitus, and Heidegger (1889–1976) considered Heraclitus a foundational thinker in Western philosophy.

The hallmarks of Heraclitus's philosophy are the unity of opposites and the concept of change, or flux. "The path up and down are one and the same."[24] From all things arises the one, and from the one all things.[25]

In his view, all things come into being by conflict of opposites, and the sum of things ("the whole") flows like a stream. "What opposes unites; the finest harmony stems from things held in tension. All things come into existence through conflict (of opposites)."[26]

Heraclitus further illustrated his concept by observing the cyclical nature of opposites—over time, opposites change into each other: "Cold things warm, warm cools; wet dries, parched moistens."[27]

Pythagoras and the Pythagoreans (c. 570–495 BCE)

The Pythagoreans believed that reality could be understood through mathematical relationships and binary oppositions. The Pythagorean school had a table of opposites—one of

23 G. W. F. Hegel, *Lectures on the History of Philosophy*, trans. E. S. Haldane (Kegan Paul, Trench, Trübner & Co., 1892), vol. 1, 279.

24 "The Fragments of Heraclitus," DK22 B60, https://heraclitusfragments.com/B60/index.html.

25 Paraphrase from Heraclitus's fragments, particularly DK22 B10 and DK22 B50. https://heraclitusfragments.com/B10/index.html, https://heraclitus-fragments.com/B50/index.html

26 "The Fragments of Heraclitus," DK22 B8, https://heraclitusfragments.com/B8/index.html. Parentheses added.

27 "The Fragments of Heraclitus," DK22 B126, https://heraclitusfragments.com/B126/index.html.

the earliest recorded attempts to categorize the world into a set of fundamental dualities.

- limited (Peras) vs. unlimited (Apeiron)
- odd vs. even
- one vs. many
- right vs. left
- male vs. female
- rest vs. motion
- straight vs. curved
- light vs. dark
- good vs. evil
- square vs. oblong

These opposites represented the tension between order (limited) and chaos (unlimited), with harmony arising from their reconciliation.

Empedocles (c. 494–434 BCE)

Empedocles said that the universe is governed by 2 opposing forces: love (*philia*), a force that unites elements; and strife (*neikos*), a force that separates them. These complementary forces drive the cycles of creation and destruction, ensuring balance in the cosmos.

Anaximander (c. 610–546 BCE)

Anaximander viewed the universe as originating from the apeiron (the boundless or infinite), which contains opposing qualities like hot and cold, wet and dry. These opposites interact in cycles, maintaining balance through mutual compensation.

Sophists (5th and 4th centuries BCE)

Sophists like Protagoras (c. 490–420 BCE) emphasized the relativity of opposites, similar to Zhuangzi in China, who developed similar ideas during the same historical period. Opposites like good and evil or just and unjust depend on perspective, challenging the concept of absolute dualities.

Stoicism (c. 300 BCE onwards)

The Stoics embraced the interplay of opposites as part of the Logos, the rational principle organizing the universe. In their view, opposites in life—like pain and pleasure, life and death—are necessary parts of a rational and harmonious universe. Wisdom involves accepting this interplay with equanimity.

Same Law, Many Names

The law of duality has been understood and expressed differently across cultures and philosophical traditions, reflecting diverse perspectives on the complementary opposites. Below are a handful to give you an overview.

Ancient Greece

- Heraclitus: unity of opposites
- Pythagoras: table of opposites
- Plato: dialectic (the highest form of knowledge)
- Neoplatonism (Plotinus): the one and the many

Mystical Traditions

- Hermes Trismegistus: law of polarity
- Kabbalah: tree of life (opposing sefirot)
- Alchemy: dissolve and coagulate

Eastern Philosophy

- Chinese: yin and yang (Tao)
- Hindu: dwanda (pairs of opposites)
- Buddhist: Madhyamaka (middle way between extremes)

Western Philosophy & Science

- Jung: mystery of conjunction
- Hegel: dialectics (thesis-antithesis-synthesis)
- Bohr: complementarity principle

Despite different names, all describe the fundamental principle that opposites are interconnected and complementary aspects of a greater whole.

The Law of Duality in Science: How We Perceive it Today

What ancient philosophers observed over millennia, modern science has not only confirmed but also expanded upon, delving deeper and bringing these ideas to new levels of understanding. In the following paragraphs, I will provide a few key reference points to illustrate how the law of duality manifests in nature, biology, mathematics, physics, and chemistry, offering a bridge between ancient wisdom and contemporary scientific understanding.

I won't delve into equal detail for each of the universal laws in this book, as my goal is to keep it concise and practical, focusing on application rather than extensive theory. There are 2 reasons why I expanded on the theoretical side for the law of duality. First, it is the most universal of all the laws (according to Hegel and Durant), underpinning countless phenomena across disciplines and cultures. Secondly, I aim to use this law as an example to demonstrate what history and science can reveal about the broader concept of universal laws. Through this focused exploration, we gain insight not only into the law of duality, but also into the timeless interplay between ancient observation and modern discovery.

Nature

In nature, duality is everywhere. Seasons change from summer to winter, tides rise and fall, half of the earth has day while half has night. These cycles maintain equilibrium. Ecosystems that rely on the balance between predators and prey are a great example of the law of duality in nature.

In 2023, on my way to Antarctica, I visited Tierra del Fuego, the southernmost part of Argentina—one of the most beautiful places I've ever seen. The scenery is stunning, and you'll be glad you took my advice if you decide to visit. They call it "the end of the world" because it is the southernmost city, the closest to Antarctica.

During this visit, I learned that beavers were artificially introduced to Tierra del Fuego in 1946 as part of a government initiative. Their intention was to stimulate the fur trade industry. At the time, beaver fur was considered valuable, and there was hope that the beavers would thrive and provide a sustainable resource for the region.

But the decision-makers underestimated the potential environmental impact. The ecosystem in Tierra del Fuego is significantly different from the beaver's native habitat in North America. Twenty pairs of Canadian beavers were initially released, but without natural predators in the region, the population exploded. Today, their numbers are estimated to be over 100,000.

Beavers have caused significant damage to the native forests, particularly the Nothofagus (southern beech) trees, which did not evolve to withstand beaver activity. Their dams have disrupted water flow, leading to changes in wetland ecosystems and loss of biodiversity.

The fur trade did not develop as anticipated and efforts to control the beaver population now cost a fortune. The scale of their spread, however, has made it an impossible task. The situation serves as a great example for what predator-prey balance means for the ecosystem.

Imagine gazelles. If they were to go without any predators for a while, they would become overweight and highly vulnerable. A predator without prey faces starvation, severe weight loss, and can't maintain fitness. A balance of prey and predator results in normal weight and maximum fitness.

The balance between prey and predator is maintained in a seemingly oscillating pattern through their natural cycle. The predator-prey cycle demonstrates how populations of predators and prey interact and influence each other's growth. As predator numbers increase, prey populations decline, leading to a decrease in predators.

Nature is trying to teach us that maximum growth, development, and fitness all occur at the border of support and challenge (prey and predator).

Biology

In a healthy adult human body, 50 to 70 billion cells are estimated to die each day through apoptosis, and a roughly equal number are created through mitosis. The balance between mitosis (cell birth) and apoptosis (programmed cell death) ensures that the body maintains tissue homeostasis, or equilibrium, in terms of the number of cells. This equilibrium maintains the body's stability and optimal function, unless disrupted by disease or injury.

This balance preserves tissue integrity and function. Disruption of this equilibrium—such as excessive cell proliferation or insufficient apoptosis—can lead to diseases like cancer. Apoptosis also serves to eliminate old or damaged cells, making room for healthy new ones and sustaining proper cellular function.

During high-growth periods—such as childhood, adolescence, pregnancy, or recovery from injury—the body temporarily shifts the balance between cell birth and cell death to support expansion and repair. Once the growth phase ends, the system shifts back to the balanced or homeostatic state.

Other examples of complementary opposites that maintain a perfect balance in biology are anabolism and catabolism, alkalinity and acidity, reduction and oxidation, blastic and clastic, parasympathetic and sympathetic.

Physics

In physics, the concept of pairs of opposites can be observed across the entire spectrum of existence, from the smallest subatomic particles to the largest known structures in the universe. At the subatomic level, we see this duality in positrons and electrons, positive and negative charges, and even the wave-particle duality. On a larger scale, it manifests in phenomena such as the north and south magnetic poles. Even the largest structures known, the Laniakea and Perseus-Pisces superclusters, look like a gigantic magnet, reflecting this universal principle of opposites.[28]

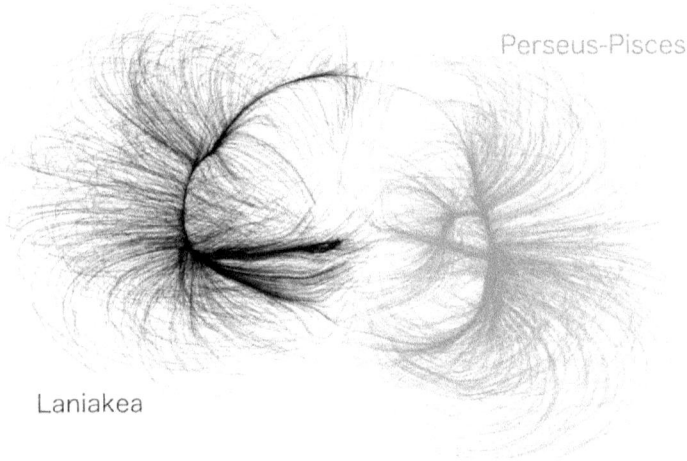

Perseus-Pisces

Laniakea

In 1687, Isaac Newton published *Principia* and marked a pivotal moment in science, laying the groundwork for modern physics and engineering. In this book he formulated the third law of motion: "For every action, there is an equal and opposite reaction."

---

28 Tsaghkyan, *Laniakea and Perseus–Pisces.png*, Wikimedia Commons, last modified November 29, 2019, https://commons.wikimedia.org/wiki/File:-Laniakea_and_Perseus-Pisces.png. Licensed under CC BY-SA 4.0, https://creativecommons.org/licenses/by-sa/4.0/.

Whenever a force acts in one direction, a complementary force acts on the same object in the opposite direction, at exactly the same time. This is how walking is possible: when you push backward against the ground with your foot, the ground pushes you forward with an equal and opposite force.

This is a powerful analogy for how our inner world is structured: support and challenge are always present in equal measure, no matter the situation. You may not see the other side, but it's there. Every experience carries both benefits and drawbacks, perfectly balanced, whether you recognize them or not. That's why, in the client stories you've read, I could confidently ask about the other side—because I know it's there.

Many physical laws reflect a similar idea to Newton's third law—that interactions are mutual and reciprocal. Some, like the conservation of momentum, directly rely on these principles in classical mechanics. Others, like the conservation of energy or electromagnetic laws, involve mutual exchanges but arise from different symmetries and may express reciprocity in more complex ways.

Quantum Physics

In 1928, Paul Dirac, a Nobel Prize-winning physicist, formulated the Dirac equation, which predicted the existence of antiparticles—counterparts to particles with opposite charge. This theoretical framework led to the prediction of the positron, the electron's antiparticle. Positrons have a positive charge, and electrons have a negative charge.

In 1932, Carl David Anderson, another Nobel Prize-winning physicist, experimentally discovered the positron using a cloud chamber to detect particles produced by cosmic rays, confirming Dirac's theory.[29]

In 1934, two other physicists, Gregory Breit and John Archibald Wheeler, wrote that when an electron and a positron collide, they produce photons. In other words, when negative and positive unite, they become light. This serves as a symbolic model for how the mind evolves through integration.

In the stories at the beginning of this chapter, you might have observed that when a client balanced positive and negative charges in their mind, the problem was solved and they felt lighter. Their minds went quiet and they knew what to do next. That is the equivalent of light in the Breit-Wheeler process.

Noise-Canceling Technology

One technological application of the law of duality is noise-canceling headphones. You've probably used Bose, AirPods, or other brands and already experienced the benefits of their noise-canceling feature. Here's how it works:

1. Noise detection: microphones on the device pick up external ambient sounds, such as engine noise or chatter.

2. Inverse sound waves: the device's processor generates an "inverse wave" that is the exact opposite of the noise wave (180 degrees out of phase).

---

29 "August 1932: Discovery of the Positron," *APS News*, American Physical Society, August 1, 2004. https://www.aps.org/apsnews/2004/08/discovery-positron-1932.

3. Wave cancellation: the inverse wave is played through the device's speakers, along with the desired audio. When the inverse wave meets the noise, they cancel each other out.

4. Noise reduction: the perception of the ambient noise is reduced or eliminated, allowing the listener to hear only the desired sound.

Of course, this technology is most effective for consistent, low-frequency noises, like airplane engines or air conditioning, and less effective for irregular, high-frequency noises. But it illustrates how pairs of opposites cancel each other on a very practical level, with a device that some of us use daily.

Mathematics

Mathematics was regarded throughout history as the universal language. Galileo (1564–1642) famously stated, "The book of nature is written in the language of mathematics." Probably nowhere is the law of duality more obvious than in mathematics. Here are just 5 mathematical examples of complementary opposites, though the list could go on and on:

1. Positive and Negative Numbers

Positive numbers represent values above zero, while negative numbers represent values below zero, often balancing each other.

2. Addition and Subtraction

Addition combines quantities, while subtraction removes or separates them.

3. Multiplication and Division

Multiplication scales a number up, while division scales it down.

4. Symmetry and Asymmetry

Symmetry involves balance and equivalence, while asymmetry describes imbalance or lack of equivalence.

5. Even and Odd Numbers

Even numbers are divisible by 2, while odd numbers leave a remainder of 1 when divided by 2.

One day-to-day application of mathematics is accounting, where you'll find dualities everywhere: debit and credit, assets and liabilities, profit and loss, etc. Each of these pairs shows how accounting systems are built on dual structures that mirror the law of duality: order, clarity, and truth arise from the interaction of opposites. The very words *balance*, *equity*, *reconciliation*, and so on are not just technical terms— they express a philosophy of wholeness arising from the integration of polarities.

At the heart of accounting lies the fundamental equation: assets = liabilities + equity. This means that everything a company owns (assets) must be financed either by borrowing money (liabilities) or through the owner's investment (equity). Every financial transaction affects at least 2 accounts in a way that keeps this equation in balance. For example, if a company takes out a loan, both its cash (asset) and its liabilities increase. This double-entry system ensures accuracy and consistency in financial records, helping businesses maintain a clear picture of their financial health.

Chemistry

Chemistry also is grounded in the principle of balance, with the idea of complementary opposites at its foundation. From the dynamic interplay of acids and bases, to the simultaneous processes of oxidation and reduction—opposing forces govern nearly every chemical interaction. These opposites work together to create harmony and drive the natural processes that sustain life and shape the material world. Whether it's the attraction between cations and anions forming ionic bonds, the energy exchange between endothermic and exothermic reactions, or the delicate equilibrium between reactants and products, complementary opposites are omnipresent in chemistry.

Conclusion

The law of duality, or the pair of complementary opposites, is so deeply ingrained in the fabric of reality that it extends into every branch of science. Physics thrives on the balance between forces like action and reaction, potential and kinetic energy, or matter and antimatter. Biology reveals dualities in life and death, mitosis and apoptosis, or predator and prey relationships. Even the social sciences grapple with opposites like cooperation and competition or order and chaos. As Will Durant observed in Hegel's thinking, duality is "the most universal of all principles," illustrating that everything exists in a delicate interplay of contrasts. I could offer examples from any field—be it geology, astronomy, or computer science—and uncover examples of this fundamental truth, demonstrating its profound and universal relevance to understanding the world around us. What makes this principle so powerful is its constancy—it holds true whether you're modeling ecosystems, decoding DNA, or designing algorithms. The deeper you investigate, the more it becomes clear: duality is not a flaw in the system, but its very foundation.

Practical Application

Take a moment and write down your insights about the law of duality so far. Use the questions below as inspiration, or explore your own reflections freely.

- What are 3 key takeaways from the last 3 chapters that had a deep impact on your life?
- What can you apply now from what you've learned?
- If you could shift your perception about one difficult experience from your past, what would it be?
- Who are the people closest to you who might benefit from learning about the law of duality?

CHAPTER 4

THE LAW OF REFLECTION

The seer, the seeing, and the seen are the same.
— Advaita Vedanta (Hindu philosophy)

The Ritz-Carlton and the Law of Reflection

The Ritz-Carlton Hotel Company was officially formed in the United States in 1983. The Ritz-Carlton name had a long tradition in Europe, tied to the legendary Ritz hotels in Paris and London from the late 19th century.

From the outset, it was clear that Ritz-Carlton positioned itself as a luxury hotel chain, where the nightly rate often exceeded the average monthly salary of its employees. You might imagine that this disparity between the guests and staff showed up in subtle but significant ways. Guests sensed an undercurrent of discomfort or hesitation in the service. Employees, often intimidated by the wealth and status of the clientele, defaulted to overly formal or mechanical inter-actions—avoiding natural, warm engagement. Their body language appeared tense, their smiles seemed forced, and their overly deferential demeanor overdid it—all reflecting the fear of making mistakes or drawing negative attention.

This lack of confidence created an awkward dynamic. The service, though polished, felt transactional rather than gen-uinely hospitable. Guests missed the warmth of authentic connection, and employees felt disconnected from the luxury experience they were expected to deliver. Leader-ship struggled to address this complex problem.

One day, Horst Schulze, the co-founder and president of Ritz-Carlton, introduced a revolutionary idea encapsulated in a slogan that would redefine the company's culture and the perception of the service industry worldwide: "We are ladies and gentlemen, serving ladies and gentlemen."[30]

Knowingly or unknowingly, Shulze used the law of reflection and gave employees a new identity and sense of purpose. The slogan conveyed that employees possessed the same dignity and worth as the guests they served. By seeing their own value reflected in their interactions, employees were encouraged to treat themselves and their roles with equal respect and honor.

This was not merely a slogan; it became a guiding principle. Ritz-Carlton began referring to staff as "ladies and gentle-men" and empowered every employee, regardless of role, to spend up to $2000 to resolve a guest's issue without needing management approval. This extraordinary trust

---

30 Horst Schulze, *Excellence Wins: A No-Nonsense Guide to Becoming the Best in a World of Compromise*, with Ken Blanchard and Dean Merrill (Zondervan, 2019), 11–13.

underscored the company's belief in its employees' profes-sionalism and judgment, aligning perfectly with the slogan.

The impact of this phrase was transformative. It became a defining aspect of Ritz-Carlton's identity, setting a new benchmark in luxury hotels. But the ripple effects went beyond the company itself. It elevated the global perception of the service industry, framing it as a noble and dignified profession. This story illustrates the level of efficiency and effectiveness individuals can achieve when they apply the universal laws.

Definition of the Law of Reflection

The law of reflection states that

everything you perceive in others exists within you.

Whatever you observe in others, you have in yourself. This applies specifically to traits—you wouldn't be able to identify a trait in someone else if that same trait didn't already reside within you. The same is true when you're perceiving someone doing or not doing something, as you will see later in this chapter.

A fascinating parallel comes from a legend about a group of indigenous people who were present when Christopher Columbus arrived in Latin America. It's said that a shaman stood on the coast, pointing out the ships on the horizon to others. "Look, look," he might have said, pointing to the floating objects. Yet, the people around him couldn't see them. Why? They had no mental framework for such vessels—they had never encountered or imagined ships before. According to the legend, they couldn't perceive the ships until they came close enough for the conquistadors to land, forcing the reality into their awareness.

Similarly, when you look outside yourself and see something—a trait, a behavior, a quality—you can only perceive it because it already exists within you. This is significant because it impacts your personal growth. The law of reflection can either hinder or propel your development. By understanding and applying this law, you can unlock or accelerate your growth.

When you resent others, it's because you're missing information and are partly unaware of aspects of your own perception. Often, this judgement stems from one of two things: (1) You are too proud to admit that what you see in them is also in you, or (2) You are too humble to admit that what you see in them is also in you.

When you're too proud to admit that what you judge in others also exists within you, you judge them negatively, and you place them in a pit. This might show itself in phrases like, "I never do that," "I am not like that," or "I don't have that." For instance, if you see someone lying, you might say, "I never lied," "I don't lie," or "I'm not a liar."

Conversely, when you're too humble to admit that what you admire in others also exists within you, you judge them positively, placing them on a pedestal. This often sounds like, "I'm not like that," "I cannot do that," "I could never do that," or "I don't have that." For example, if you witness someone excelling at public speaking, you might think, "I can't do that," "I'll never be able to do that," or "That's just not me."

In both cases, the underlying dynamic is the same: you deny aspects of yourself that you see reflected in others. Whether through pride or humility, this denial limits your self-aware-ness and growth as we saw in the Ritz-Carlton story.

First Question to Apply the Law of Reflection:
Where Do You Have the Same or Similar Trait?

Five years ago I worked with Lily, an entrepreneur who owned a production business. She had a serious problem: her employees were stealing from her. They took raw mate-rials, pocketed money, sold products and kept the cash, and so on. This had been going on for a long time and it frustrated her deeply, both personally and professionally.

Lily told me how much it hurt, how it pushed all her buttons, and how it made her feel like she couldn't trust people anymore. Every theft felt like a personal betrayal. It was exhausting. She was constantly on edge, waiting for the next time it would happen.

She tried everything to stop it—installed cameras, did surprise checks, fired employees who got caught, even consulted security experts. But nothing worked. No matter what she did, they always found a new way. It became an endless, draining cycle.

When we started working together I asked Lily, "Can you think of a time when you stole something?" She immediately said no. She swore she had never stolen in her life. I noticed her body language. She tensed up, her jaw tightened.

So I rephrased the question: "Can you think of a time when you took something that wasn't yours? In what areas of life do you currently steal?" She got frustrated. "No! I told you, I never steal," she said defensively.

I shifted gears. "Have you always reported the salaries you paid your employees?" She hesitated. Reluctantly she admitted, "Not always."

I nodded. "So, in a way, you didn't fully report to the state—and that means you stole from them." She exhaled and gave a faint smile. "Yeah, I see what you mean."

I continued. "Have you declared all the bonuses you've given?" Another pause. "No," she answered.

"So, you didn't pay taxes on those bonuses. That means you stole from the state, right?" She sighed, then laughed. "Yes." Now she understood where this was going.

Since Lily worked with family, I asked, "Have you ever taken advantage of them? Maybe avoided officially registering their salaries or bonuses because they were family? In other words, did you steal from them *and* the state?" Another pause. Then finally, "Yes."

One by one, she uncovered moments where she had done the very thing she resented in others. And then, after a long silence, she suddenly blurted out—"Holy smokes! I have this trait too! In equal measure, just like you said—both quantitatively and qualitatively." It was a powerful realization—one she hadn't expected.

And then, something incredible happened. Her employees stopped stealing.

She didn't install more cameras. She didn't tighten security. She didn't fire anyone. She simply changed something inside herself—and the whole situation shifted.

Once Lily saw that she also had the trait she was judging in others, the dynamic transformed. Trust and accountability naturally rebuilt themselves. And suddenly, she was no longer fighting a losing battle with her own team.

Reflection and Deflection in Physics

In physics, reflection and deflection are terms used to describe different behaviors of light when encountering surfaces or objects. Perfect reflection occurs when light strikes a mirror and bounces back without distortion, showing a clear and true image. Deflection occurs when light strikes a surface and is scattered or redirected, often due to irregularities or interference. This scattering prevents a clear image from forming.

Imagine standing in front of a clear, smooth mirror (reflective): you see yourself as you are. Now imagine standing in front of a cracked or fogged-up surface (deflective): your image is distorted or missing altogether.

Similar to physics, there are 2 types of awareness: reflective awareness and deflective awareness.

Reflective awareness means authenticity and a willingness to look directly at oneself. It is about admitting that what we see in others, we also have in ourselves. The client in the previous section took a moment of reflective awareness and asked herself when she had stolen and from whom. This is why she was able to grow.

Deflective awareness means inauthenticity and involves avoiding, distorting, or diverting attention from one's true self. If she had refused to see when she had stolen in her personal or professional life, she wouldn't have seen that growth or transformation.

Let's talk about efficiency. The business world is obsessed with efficiency, and there are many books on the topic—but let's see what we can learn from physics and mathematics. The French mathematician Pierre de Fermat demonstrated the principle of least time all the way back in 1662. Fermat's principle states that light travels between 2 points along the path that requires the least time.

This path may not always be the shortest distance geometrically, but it is the one that minimizes the overall travel time based on the medium it traverses. In other words, the most efficient path is not always a straight line but the path that minimizes the action—a concept from the principle of least action in physics. The light's behavior aligns with the natural tendency of systems to optimize energy and time.

When you break the law of reflection, efficiency becomes impossible. Like in the Ritz-Carlton's story, the imbalance hurt the whole atmosphere—employees avoided personal touches, making the lavish experience feel inauthentic and strained. Struggle and resistance arise when we violate the principle of least time. Depending on your level of reflective or deflective awareness in any given moment, life can either feel difficult, hard, and full of struggle—or it can flow with ease, inspiration, and clarity.

The Law of Reflection in Philosophy and Mystic Traditions

Advaita Vedanta, a prominent school of Hindu philosophy dating back to 1500 BCE, invites individuals to see beyond the illusions of separation and recognize the infinite, undivided reality of existence. They have a beautiful famous saying: "The seer, the seeing, and the seen are the same." The phrase encapsulates the idea that in the ultimate reality (brahman), there is no distinction between the observer (seer), the process of observation (seeing), and the object observed (seen). All are manifestations of the same unified consciousness. Similar concepts can be found in other mystical traditions globally, from Zen Buddhism to Sufism, where the oneness of existence is a recurring theme.

In the New Testament, Romans 2:1 says, "You, therefore, have no excuse, you who pass judgment on someone else, for at whatever point you judge another, you are condemning yourself, because you who pass judgment do the same things."[31] The Bible has 4 places where it says "you shall love your neighbor as yourself,"[32] pointing out the mirror-type equality between self and nonself.

In the Islamic tradition and Sufi teachings, a similar saying is attributed to the Prophet Muhammad: "He who knows himself knows his Lord." According to the philosopher Avicenna (Ibn Sina, 10th–11th century) the meaning of the inscription at the Temple of Apollo at Delphi was "know thyself, O man, and you will know God."[33]

Rumi, the poet and the Sufi mystic, beautifully said, "You are not a drop in the ocean. You are the entire ocean in a drop." This timeless wisdom reminds us that self-knowledge

31 New International Version (NIV).

32 This biblical command is found in Leviticus 19:18, Matthew 22:39, Mark 12:31, and Luke 10:27.

33 Alexander Altmann, "The Delphic Maxim in Medieval Islam and Judaism," in *Biblical and Other Studies*, ed. Alexander Altmann (Harvard University Press, 1963), 196 232.

reveals the interconnectedness of all existence and the law of reflection.

Mirror Neurons: a Discovery through Monkeys and Peanuts

Giacomo Rizzolatti and his team set out to study how the brain controls movement at the University of Parma in the early 1990s. Using macaque monkeys, they tracked neuron activity during simple tasks like reaching for food. It was routine science—until something unexpected happened.

One day, a monkey sat still, watching a researcher pick up food. To everyone's surprise, the monkey's neurons fired as if it had performed the action itself. The team was baffled. How could neurons for movement activate when the monkey wasn't moving?

The researchers tested further and found a clear pattern: specific neurons in the monkey's brain fired not only when it performed an action, but also when it watched someone else perform the same action. These neurons didn't react to random movements—only to purposeful, goal-directed actions, like grasping food.

They realized they had discovered mirror neurons, a unique class of neurons that allowed the monkey to "mirror" the actions of others in its brain. Around 10–20 percent of the neurons studied showed this behavior, hinting at the brain's ability to understand and empathize with others' actions.

Published in 1992, the discovery reshaped neuroscience, offering insights into how we learn, empathize, and connect socially. What started as a simple experiment with monkeys and peanuts became a cornerstone in understanding the brain, showing how we truly reflect one another.[34]

We "Delegate" Positive and Negative Traits Until We Are Ready to Own Them

Mirror neurons explain how the traits we perceive in others are mirrored within ourselves. Let me illustrate this with an example involving my colleague, Jasmine.

Jasmine is someone who works tirelessly. To put it bluntly, she's obsessed with work. When I observe her and label her in this way—and let me emphasize that this is simply a label—it reveals something about my own mental processes. By identifying this trait in Jasmine, my brain is essentially engaging in the same behavior: being obsessed with work. This occurs because of mirror neurons, which replicate in us the actions and behaviors we perceive in others. In essence, whatever I see in her is simultaneously occurring within me. As Ralph Waldo Emerson said: "As I am, so I see,"[35] and "We can never say anything but what we are."[36]

A deeper nuance of this principle is tied to how our brain functions in recognizing and interpreting activities. Neural activity in certain brain areas overlaps when we act and when we observe others acting. The brain's purpose is to swiftly identify behaviors, label them, and evaluate whether

---

34 Giacomo Rizzolatti di Pellegrino et al., "Understanding Motor Events: A Neurophysiological Study," *Experimental Brain Research* 91, no. 1 (1992): 176–180.

35 Ralph Waldo Emerson, *Essays: Second Series* (James Munroe and Company, 1844), "Experience."

36 Ralph Waldo Emerson, *Essays: First Series* (James Munroe and Company, 1841), "The Over-Soul."

they pose a threat or are harmless. For instance, when I see Jasmine's dedication to work, my brain processes this information to determine whether it's something I should approach or avoid. This process helps me decide if she is a potential ally or a threat—whether to engage with her or to distance myself.

What makes this phenomenon even more profound is its spiritual implication. Mirror neurons enable us to see traits in others that we might not yet be ready to acknowledge in ourselves. This is a fundamental aspect of the law of reflection. For example, if I criticize Jasmine for being obsessed with work, it's not because I lack that trait—rather, it's because I'm not prepared to own it. At that moment, it's easier for me to "delegate" this trait to her and judge her for it than to admit its presence in myself.

This principle applies not only to the traits we criticize, but also to those we admire in others. The traits we see in others are reflections of what exists within us, whether we're ready to own them or not. Recognizing this can lead to deeper self-awareness and self-mastery, as it invites us to own all aspects of ourselves rather than projecting them onto others.

Your Own Form

In a recent webinar, I received an intriguing question: "If you see something in someone that you also recognize in yourself, can it only be tied to the past? For example, if it's related to working hard—you might observe someone who seems obsessed with work and think, 'I can clearly relate to that because in the past, when I had a job, I worked like that. But now, since I don't have a job, I don't work as much.'"

The short answer is no. The longer answer is not about past or present, but about form. The law of transformation, which we cover in the next chapter, states that you possess all traits at all times. You don't lose or gain traits—instead, the *form* in which these traits manifest changes. When we combine the law of transformation and the law of reflection, we gain deeper insight into this phenomenon.

It's very easy for the mind to say, "Look at Jasmine—she's obsessed with work." Then I might add, "Ah yes, I used to do that too, but now I don't. I don't work so many hours a day anymore."

But let's pause here. If someone were to ask, "What do you do in your free time? What occupies your thoughts?" The answer might reveal a different picture. Take my own example: even during free time, when I'm not physically at my desk, my thoughts are often consumed by work projects. I'm not actively managing them, but I'm imagining solutions or pondering a client's challenge. It's my mental obsession. When I talk to my husband, these topics dominate our conversations to the extent that I sometimes catch myself and think, "Monica, can you change the subject? You've been talking about this too much." So the trait of being obsessed with work hasn't disappeared—it's presenting itself in a different form. By the way—in my opinion, achieving a level of excellence inherently requires some degree of obsession.

In the webinar, I turned the question back to the woman who asked it and said, "So, tell us—how does your obsession with work show up now? I suspect it's no coincidence that you brought this up. Be honest—how much do you work now?" She paused and replied, "Well, at first, I was going to say that I really don't work much. But then I realized I do. I was employed until last year, but I resigned for personal reasons and recently started a consulting business. The truth is, I work many hours at home, in my home, with my kids and on my new business. So yes, my work doesn't look the same as it did before, but it's there."

This exchange beautifully illustrates the interplay of the law of reflection and the law of transformation (see chapter 5). Our traits persist, but their forms change. Recognizing this can help us better understand ourselves and others.

Second Question to Apply the Law of Reflection: *When and Where Did You Do the Same in Your Own Form?*

A few years ago, I worked with a client from New York who owned a home nursing service business, which she had built from the ground up. We'll call her Julia. She had a sharp mind for business and a knack for finding creative solutions. Julia scheduled a video call to talk through one of the biggest hurdles she was facing at work.

Her biggest challenge was that her nurses often quit without any warning. These were individuals she had hired and invested heavily in, providing professional training—only for them to eventually lose interest and quit. They found the work too demanding.

As Julia opened up to me, I could see that her face was tense, her lips tight. "I don't know what to do," she said. "Every day, I'm terrified someone's going to leave. When a co-worker asks to talk, my first thought is that they're resigning. If the tone of a message shifts even a little, I brace myself for bad news. And if someone takes a day off without notice, I can't help but imagine they're not coming back and I'm left without any help."

"It sounds exhausting," I said.

She sighed deeply, her shoulders sagging. "I hold things in. I won't say what I need to say because I'm afraid of saying the wrong thing. Then, when I finally do speak up, it's too much. I say things I regret. Or I explode at home, and my kids and husband get the brunt of my anger."

It was clear that these fear and anger cycles were taking a toll on both her business and her personal life. So we started working through it.

"Let's take a look at how you're doing this in your own particular form," I suggested. "How are you abandoning people, professionally speaking?" Julia looked confused at first. "What do you mean? I don't abandon anyone."

"Think about your clients. Have you ever given up on a client because they wanted something more complex or demanded more of your time?" She paused, then hesitated. "Well, yeah. Some clients ask for things that are hard to manage, and I've let them go. Or, if they moved too far away, I would tell them that we can't travel so far."

"Okay," I said, nodding. "So, you have quit working with them, which can be a form of abandonment. Now, let's talk about your nurses. Have you ever abandoned any of them?" She shifted uncomfortably in her chair. "I don't know. Maybe? I haven't fired anyone."

I interrupted, "No need to fire anyone. Just think about when you've given up on a colleague, even without doing anything outwardly. When have you mentally abandoned them?" It took a moment, but then she spoke slowly, "I guess when I stopped assigning some of them clients. I just didn't feel like they were reliable anymore, so I stopped giving them work." And then her face flushed with realization. "Oh, wow! I didn't even see it, but I've been doing the same thing."

I nodded, encouraging her to keep going. "When you do that, you're essentially punishing them, right? You stop giving them work—stop including them in your system. You push them away without saying anything."

"Exactly," she admitted, her voice quieter. "I never saw it that way before. But you're right. I've been abandoning people. Not just at work, either—my family members too."

Then tears welled up in Julia's eyes and she softly added, "I abandoned my grandmother. When I moved to New York, I left her behind. She couldn't come with me, and I didn't think much of it at the time." We paused, silence stretching between us. I let the silence settle before guiding her through the next step.

"Let's apply the law of duality," I said. "It's time to dissolve the emotional charges and negative judgments you had about yourself abandoning people. What benefits did your grandmother gain from you leaving? What benefits did she get from that abandonment?"

Julia furrowed her brow, processing the question. "Well, I remember that she started being more active in her own life. She stopped being as reliant on me. She began to meet her friends more often. She even started travelling with them."

"And what about the nurses?" I asked. "What benefits did they gain from you 'quitting on them' or abandoning them—no longer giving them clients?" After a few moments of reflection, she answered, "Mona secured a job near her home, which was a priority for her. Emily pursued her dream of working at the hospital. As for Miriam, she took the opportunity to prepare for her wedding."

Julia sat back slightly, her shoulders no longer rigid, her hands resting still in her lap. The tightness around her mouth had eased, replaced by a look of quiet thoughtfulness. She exhaled, slowly and steadily, letting this new understanding sink in. When she finally met my gaze, there was a new light in her eyes. We worked through the benefits and disadvantages, and slowly, the emotional charge around the situation started to dissolve. It was clear that she saw both sides.

That's why in our work, we use specific protocols to maximize efficiency. While individual questions are powerful, linking them together into a structured process is where the true transformation occurs.

After Julia saw that she, too, had abandoned people both personally and professionally, the major change in her life was that she began leading her organization with clarity and strength. She no longer feared that clients or employees would leave her.

She shared her experience with me a few months later. "I've set strong boundaries with my clients and colleagues now," she said. "If someone isn't doing their job properly, I don't hesitate anymore. I say, 'This isn't working professionally, so we'll stop here.' I've brought structure and order to my business, and it's paying off. My client flow has increased by almost 50 percent in the past 6 months."

By using the law of reflection to face her own fears and take responsibility for her actions, Julia had transformed both her business and her personal life.

Isabella Finds Her Own Form

I presented a special webinar on the law of reflection in 2024. It started off as a typical webinar. The virtual room buzzed with energy as nearly 500 attendees logged in, eager to learn and share. Among them was Isabella—a beautiful, middle-aged woman whose courage to openly discuss her struggles left a lasting impression on me. Her question came early on, striking a chord that resonated deeply with many in the audience.

"I have a problem when I see people around me drinking a lot," she began timidly. "I never drink. So, I don't understand. How can I own this trait, since I don't drink alcohol?" I nodded, understanding the weight of her words. "Do you want to work on this topic a little bit?" I asked, smiling. "You're not going to like it."

Isabella smiled. "Not a problem—and yes, I want to work on it," she said. I continued, "Okay, great. Can you think of someone who drinks and who pushes your buttons? Someone whose behavior really bothers you?"

Her answer came quickly. "Yes."

"Can you give me that person's name?"

"Sam, my husband," she said without hesitation. From there, we dove into the heart of her discomfort. I asked her to detail what specifically bothered her about Sam's drinking.

"The way he behaves when he is drunk," she replied, after giving it some thought.

"Can you be more specific?" I asked.

"He transforms into someone else," she said, frustration evident in her voice.

"Be even more specific," I encouraged. She hesitated but then said, "He uses violent language. He listens to stupid music, which I hate. And he says things that hurt me."

"Out of all of these," I asked, "what upsets you the most?"

"The last one," she admitted, with a trace of sadness in her voice. "He says things that really hurt me."

We drilled down further, unraveling the root of her pain. Was it that Sam couldn't control himself, or that he didn't filter his words? Isabella clarified that it was his lack of control that bothered her most.

"Okay," I said. "Now, I'm going to ask you to give me 3 specific moments when you weren't able to control yourself and said things that hurt others." Isabella paused, and I could sense her internal resistance. "I judged my former spouse out loud and told him he's incapable of doing anything," she finally admitted, her tone reflective.

"Are you thinking about a specific moment?" I asked.

"Yes," she said quietly. The change in her energy was palpable.

THE 7 UNIVERSAL LAWS

"Great," I said. "Now, another moment, please."

She began recounting instances where she had said things that hurt her ex-husband, her children, her sister, and even herself. Each moment where she identified herself doing the same thing brought her closer to the realization that the traits and actions she judged in Sam were ones she had also displayed in different contexts, particularly with her children.

Recognizing her brave vulnerability in front of so many watching eyes and wanting to lighten the mood, I joked, "So, are there any perfect parents here who have never said something they regretted to their kids? No? Well, Isabella, looks like we're both sinners, but hey, at least we've got company!" The lightheartedness helped her relax, because the work she was doing was far from easy.

As we progressed, Isabella's defenses softened. I could see her shoulders relax and her posture shift. She brought up moments where she lost control of her emotions, hurting others with harsh words, and even reproaching herself. Each example she recalled of her own loss of control and hurtful words chipped away at the pedestal she had placed herself on while simultaneously putting Sam in a pit.

"How do you feel now about owning Sam's trait—that you say things that hurt and can't control yourself?" I asked after a series of answers. "I'm at about 75 percent," she admitted with a trace of relief in her voice.

"Good," I said. "Keep going. Identify more moments. It's not about blaming yourself, but owning the traits you see in him 100 percent. This process helps balance your perception and reduces judgement." After a few more answers, she finished the exercise and owned the trait 100 percent.

As we wrapped up, Isabella expressed her gratitude. "I'm really thankful that I was able to do this exercise," she said, her eyes bright. "It helped me calm that charge down. Sam makes an effort to control his drinking, but it had gotten to the point where even the sight of alcohol triggered me. This exercise just helped me dissolve a big part of the charge."

I smiled, touched by her honesty. "Thank you for your courage, Isabella. By sharing your story, you've helped everyone here see that we all share traits we judge in others. This is how we grow."

The Keys to Greatness

My colleague and FTP specialist, Dana, worked with a client 6 years ago who was an entrepreneur and owned an IT company. Let's call him Simon. Their initial focus was to eliminate the limiting beliefs that were keeping him stuck in the pattern of needing to be the smartest one in the room. Once they made progress on that, they moved on to a protocol we call "the keys to greatness."

"So, let's talk about someone you admire," Dana began. "Who would you like to model for this process?" Simon thought for a moment before answering. "Elon Musk. He's incredibly innovative, and he has the ability to bring those innovations to life in a big way."

"Alright," Dana said. "Now, here are the key questions I want you to think about: What do you admire about Elon Musk, what do you judge about him, and how do those traits also show up in you?" Simon paused, reflecting on the question. "Well, Musk has innovative ideas that he believes in and capitalizes on. I really admire that."

"Excellent," Dana responded. "Let's explore that a bit. When in your own life have you had innovative ideas, believed in them, and capitalized on them?" At first, Simon seemed unsure, but Dana encouraged him to dig deeper. "Think about moments when you've had ideas that felt new and bold."

Slowly, he began to piece things together. "I've had several smaller products that were successful. And there were business opportunities I pursued, ones that paid off. I also recognized the potential of certain funding opportunities, and I went after them. That worked too."

Dana smiled. "That's a great start. Now, think about what shifted for you when you realized the potential of funding opportunities." Simon's eyes lit up. "I see it now. The moment I chose to partner with another business that specialized in securing funds—it opened up so many possibilities. I approached government institutions with a plan to upgrade their IT systems, and we secured the funds to make it happen."

Dana nodded. "Well done! You saw that using funding was a key to implementing innovative ideas. And it led you to the same kind of impact that Musk has—upgrading outdated systems and implementing these changes on a larger scale." The entrepreneur leaned back in his chair with a new light in his eyes. "Wow, I never thought of it like that. I actually have the same trait as Elon Musk, in my own form." This realization made a significant impact on his life.

Simon later told Dana that it was the tipping point for him. After he made that realization, he was able to leap from deals worth hundreds of thousands of dollars to deals worth millions.

From my perspective, the most powerful change had occurred when he started to own the same traits that he admired in Elon Musk. Borrowing a metaphor from physics, we could say he collapsed the time and space separating his current reality from the one he wanted to manifest. Through the "keys to greatness" process, he was able to shrink time and space, and it was as if a great door had opened, enabling him to make a significant professional leap.

Why Forgiveness Doesn't Work

For my husband, Stefan, the law of reflection is the most effective law. Whatever emotional charge he is working on, it calms down pretty quickly when he sees that he also displays the same trait, action, or inaction in his own form. His mind becomes more flexible, and lets go of his previous narrative more quickly.

I've encountered a category of people, however, for whom the law of reflection is less effective unless it's combined with the law of duality.

When I first met my client Emma, she told me, "I have forgiven my mother." When I hear statements like this, I instantly become aware that the healing process isn't complete in that case. Why? Because our modern understanding of forgiveness is a form of moral hypocrisy. It places us in a position of superiority, as if forgiveness is something we "grant" to others from a seat of judgement.

In Emma's case, forgiveness of her mother essentially meant she believed her mother had been "bad" to her. Forgiving made Emma the hero in the story. Consequently, there were disowned parts. Emma was not willing to own the same traits she judged in her mother, nor did she want to acknowledge that her mother embodied both positives and negatives in equal measure.

Although Emma said "I have forgiven my mother," in reality she still harbored resentments toward her mom because her mind was not balanced—the negative and positive charges were still there. As a result, she could not bear to be in the presence of her mother for more than 2 days, and she would usually end up storming out of her parents' home most times she visited. Her mother still pushed her buttons to the maximum, and forgiveness didn't help her resolve her charges.

At a more subtle level, modern understanding of forgiveness comes from a position of superiority where we refuse to own the traits we judge in others. When people "forgive" they use rational expressions like, "we must forgive and move on," "they did the best they could," "that's how she was raised," and "I'm a good person, and I forgive them, but they still did something wrong." So the negative label remains, and they don't see the complementary opposites integrated.

I've had quite a few Christian clients who were so attached to the idea of forgiveness that it became nearly impossible for them to integrate the duality of positive and negative, good and evil, and find balance. They viewed the negative as separate from the positive, not realizing that true perfection lies in the integration of both. They needed to separate good from evil because, without that division, their limited concept of God as "all positive" and the devil as "all negative" no longer made sense. But opposites co-create one another—if the devil doesn't exist, neither does God. They placed good and evil into separate categories so they could see themselves as "good." This mindset trapped them in a victim mentality. They cast themselves as the hero of their story, which required someone else to be the villain. Yet the hero and the villain co-create each other, like 2 sides of Newton's third law—every action triggering an equal and opposite reaction.

The Bible makes it clear that God is not solely positive. Many passages in both the Old and New Testaments highlight God's dual nature in His relationship with humanity, balancing blessings and challenges, positives and negatives.

For example, Exodus 4:11 states, "The LORD said to him, 'Who gave human beings their mouths? Who makes them deaf or mute? Who gives them sight or makes them blind? Is it not I, the LORD?'"

Similarly, 1 Samuel 2:6–7 reads, "The LORD brings death and makes alive; he brings down to the grave and raises up. The LORD sends poverty and wealth; he humbles and he exalts."

And in Matthew 10:34–36, Jesus says: "Do not suppose that I have come to bring peace to the earth. I did not come to bring peace, but a sword. For I have come to turn 'a man against his father, a daughter against her mother, a daughter-in-law against her mother-in-law—a man's enemies will be the members of his own household."[37]

---

37 New International Version (NIV).

Despite these verses, there are Christians who believe that God is exclusively positive while attributing all negativity solely to the devil. This was also the case with Emma. She couldn't balance the emotional charge with her mother because she wasn't ready to let go of the old paradigm. She still wanted to believe in good as separated from evil. She needed her mother to be bad and guilty so she could maintain a position of superiority.

The Forgotten Meaning of Forgiveness

What I said previously may seem as if I'm contradicting the Bible and that Jesus made a mistake in telling people to "forgive." But let's explore the historical context a bit deeper and see what was lost in translation.

In the Roman Empire, the Law of the Twelve Tables (451–450 BCE) was highly punitive and based on the principle of talion, commonly known as *lex talionis*. It means equal retaliation, or "an eye for an eye." For example, if someone inflicted physical harm the injured party was allowed to exact a proportional revenge. In practice, the reality was different—in the Roman Empire, violence often escalated and revenge was rarely proportional.

In Roman-occupied Israel, the Pharisees were a Jewish sect who thought they were righteous and superior to the Romans because they had an elaborate system where they restricted people from doing more harm than what was done to them. So if someone cut off someone else's finger, the Judaic legal practices ensured that the family of the person whose finger was cut only could do the exact same.

The family members could go and cut the accused person's finger but not their hand or leg.[38]

Jesus challenged the Roman and Judaic system of *lex talionis*, and if you take a closer look at the Greek meaning of the word *forgiveness* and why Jesus used it, you will discover something that might surprise you.

The word we now translate as "forgiveness" comes from the Greek word *aphiēmi* (ἀφίημι), which more accurately means "to let go." When Jesus used the word *aphiēmi*, it was to tell his followers to abandon the *lex talionis* system altogether and to simply let go—to stop viewing people as if they owe us something or deserve retaliation. In my opinion, the translation of the word *aphiēmi* as "forgive" is a weaker choice than the more literal "let go," due to the different meaning it conveys.

This principle is exemplified in the story of the woman caught in adultery. When the Pharisees brought her before Jesus, they sought to enforce the Mosaic law, which required that she be stoned to death as retribution for her actions. Yet Jesus responded to her crowd of accusers with, "Let any one of you who is without sin be the first to throw a stone at her."[39]

Jesus's statement challenged the crowd to look inward and see that what they were judging in her, they also had in themselves. He knew that once they did, they would not be

---

38 This is still very relevant today, since in 2025, certain nations incorporate elements of retributive justice that resemble *lex talionis*. For instance, countries such as Iran, Saudi Arabia, Pakistan, Nigeria, Afghanistan, Qatar, and the United Arab Emirates have legal provisions allowing for punishments mirroring the harm caused, particularly in cases of murder or bodily injury.

39 John 8:1–11. NIV.

able to pick up a stone. Through this act, Jesus dismantled the self-righteousness of those who believed they were superior. This highlights the fact that if we are honest with ourselves and balance our perceptions, we can truly "let go," seeing that what we judge in others is also in ourselves. What an amazing way to explain the law of reflection at any level throughout millennia!

Nowadays, we often say "I forgive but I won't forget." This is a perfect example of how far we've strayed from the initial understanding of letting go. We saw this in Emma's story above. Her belief that forgiveness meant being "better" than her mother kept her stuck in a cycle of resentment. She continued to have a strong emotional charge towards her mom.

As demonstrated in many of the stories already shared in these first chapters, you can't really let go unless the charge is completely neutral. The only way to truly let go is by seeing positives and negatives in equal measure, and by applying the law of duality and the law of reflection. Otherwise, your brain will still store the memory. When your perception is neutral, there is nothing to forgive and you naturally let go and move forward.

3 Principles to Apply the Law of Reflection

Life is always showing us who we are—through the people we meet, the emotions we feel, and the patterns that repeat. The law of reflection is one of the most present teachers we have. Here are 3 principles that will help you apply it more in daily life.

Principle 1: Reflection Calms Down the Judgement

When you recognize that the traits you judge in others also exist within you, in your own form but to the same extent, your thinking becomes more open and less critical. Simply becoming aware of this is often enough to help the mind let go and move forward, as we saw in Julia's and Isabella's stories above.

This principle is beautifully synthesized in the New Testament when Jesus said, "Why do you look at the speck of sawdust in your brother's eye and pay no attention to the plank in your own eye? How can you say to your brother, 'Let me take the speck out of your eye,' when all the time there is a plank in your own eye? You hypocrite, first take the plank out of your own eye, and then you will see clearly to remove the speck from your brother's eye."[40]

Principle 2: Anything You Haven't Owned Will Keep Repeating in Your Life

Owning a behavior means recognizing you possess it to the same degree you perceive it in others—100%, both in quality and quantity.

The behaviors you resent in others don't just fade. They create a reality in which you keep encountering that person and similar experiences you had with them in different forms. You'll notice the energy of that experience and the emotions you felt in relation to that individual coming back again and again in your life.

If your dad was critical and you resented him for that, it's possible you now criticize yourself—or have created a

---

40 Matthew 7:3–5, New International Version (NIV).

reality where someone else is highly critical of you. Maybe your husband is that person, maybe your boss, maybe your children.

Everything and everyone you resent will reappear in your life until you learn to love them. Narratives like, "I'm not that way" or "I would never do that" keep you stuck. To grow, you need to own them 100% and also see how they serve you and others. The moment you bring that resentment into balance, you'll start to see immediate signs and shifts in your reality—because you'll step out of the loop of negative judgment and, in doing so, change your reality.

Principle 3: Reflect Traits of the Next Level

The third principle is about moving to the next level you want to reach. For any trait you admire or resent at that level, believing you don't have it blocks you from getting there.

One of the fastest ways to grow is to recognize that the traits you admire in others are already within you. If you're unaware of this, it's like locking the door to that level. For instance, if you admire someone's financial achievements but don't see that same trait in yourself, you're directing your energy outward instead of using it to grow.

In summary, using the law of reflection for advancement means:

- Calming down your mind, resentments, and admirations through reflection.
- Owning the behaviors you resent in others, and seeing how they benefit you and others.

- Recognizing you already have the traits needed to reach your next level.

By applying these 3 principles you activate the profound power of the law of reflection, transforming it into a compass for your journey toward greater purpose and growth.

Practical Application

Here are 2 practical actions to use this information and bring it into your own life more.

1. Own a Negative Trait

Pick a trait of someone you know that you've recently judged negatively and believe you don't possess to the same extent. Translate that trait into an objective and specific action—what they did or didn't do. Here are a few examples for inspiration. Keep in mind that these are subjective, so feel free to create your own versions.

- Laziness: postpones doing what I ask and watches TV instead.
- Arrogance: dismisses what others say without listening.
- Neediness: needs my help or others' help to achieve certain results.
- Aggressiveness: hit me or imposed their opinion by yelling at me.
- Oversensitivity: reacts emotionally to simple things.
- Selfishness: prioritizes their own needs over others' needs.

- Indecisiveness: delays making decisions.
- Vanity: prioritizes beauty and handbags over intellectual values.
- Coldness: doesn't express emotions, doesn't say "I love you."
- Rebelliousness: deliberately breaks the rules.

Then ask yourself: When and where did you display the same action, *in your own form*? Make sure you identify specific moments in time and space, not just "in general, I do this."

Give at least 25 answers of specific moments in the past where you displayed the same or similar action. Don't stop until you can wholeheartedly say that you possess the same trait to the same extent—both quantitatively and qualitatively—as the individual you chose.

Now, it's possible to feel guilty when you realize you've done the same thing you resented in others. To balance that perception, simply apply the law of duality by answering this question: What were the benefits for the person toward whom you expressed the action you judged? Give 7–15 responses.

2. Own a Positive Trait

Pick a trait of someone you know that you've recently admired and believe you don't possess to the same extent. Translate that trait into an objective and specific action— what they did or didn't do. Here are a few examples for inspiration. Keep in mind that these are subjective, so feel free to create your own versions.

- Patience: has patience with me when I express my emotions, without interrupting me.

- Empathy: deeply understands the emotions I'm experiencing.

- Open-mindedness: adapts easily and is eager to learn.

- Punctuality: arrives on time or completes work on time.

- Fairness: applies the same set of rules to all colleagues.

- Discipline: does what they set out to do within the time they planned.

- Confidence: expresses their ideas with certainty and provides clear explanation.

- Humility: doesn't boast about financial or academic achievements.

- Creativity: finds creative solutions to the problems they face.

- Courage: shares their opinion without fear in relation to authority figures.

Then ask yourself: When and where did you display the same action, *in your own form*? Make sure you identify specific moments in time and space, not "in general, I do this."

Give at least 25 answers of specific moments in the past where you displayed the same or similar action. Don't stop until you can wholeheartedly say that you possess the same trait to the same extent—both quantitatively and qualitatively—as the individual you chose.

Now, it's possible to feel proud when you realize you've done the same thing you admired in others. To balance that perception, simply apply the law of duality by answering this question: What were the drawbacks for the person toward whom you expressed the action you admired? Give 7–15 responses.

CHAPTER 5

THE LAW OF TRANSFORMATION

There is no grief, without relief.
— Dr. John Demartini

What My Mom Taught Me About The Law Of Transformation

My mother fell gravely ill in the spring of 2018. It came suddenly—an unforeseen storm that shook our family. By then, I had studied and worked with the law of transformation—the idea that nothing is ever truly lost, but rather transformed. However, I hadn't had the opportunity to thoroughly test it in my own life, as no close family members had passed away.

My emotions have always been very intense, and I've often spoken about how strongly I feel them. So when I received the call from the doctor, I knew I was about to face a moment that would either strengthen or challenge my understanding of transformation.

The call came one evening while I was staying with my dad in a city in the heart of Transylvania. My mom was in the hospital, and the doctor's voice carried both urgency and empathy as he informed me, "Your mother is unlikely to survive the night. If you want to be with her, now is the time." My heart tightened with fear. I was terrified of witnessing such a moment, but deep inside I knew I needed to be there. I told my dad and we made our way to the hospital.

When we arrived, my mother was already in a coma. The room was silent except for the faint hum of medical equipment. My dad and I sat by her bedside as the inevitable unfolded. With each breath she took, I felt the weight of finality settling in. Then I sensed it—her last breath. A stillness filled the room—profound and unshakable.

As the medical staff began their necessary procedures, my dad and I stepped into the hallway. When the doctor approached us with 2 nurses, his calm, empathetic demeanor struck me. His voice carried a sense of normalcy intertwined with deep empathy, a combination that mirrored my mother's own essence. It was as if, in that moment, she spoke through him, comforting us with her presence.

When we returned home, something remarkable happened. My dad prepared breakfast—something he never did for me before. He brewed coffee, set the table, and moved about the kitchen with a determination specific to my mom. It was as if he had stepped into my mother's role, embodying her spirit to provide for us in her stead. This was the first clear manifestation of the law of transformation that I could see, tangible and undeniable.

Later on, my dad had to leave for my hometown to handle administrative tasks related to my mother's passing. Left alone, I decided to seek solace in comfort food and headed to KFC. At the counter, I observed the young employee who was supposed to serve me. But instead of serving me, she flitted from task to task, opening new loops and leaving them unresolved. Her chaotic behavior was exactly how my mom behaved under pressure when she was in the kitchen.

I stood frozen for a moment, watching this stranger embody my mother's quirks so vividly. Less than 24 hours after her death, here she was again—manifested in the energy and actions of someone I'd never met. The realization left me awestruck. My mother's essence, her unique patterns and traits, continued to show up in unexpected forms.

Over the following weeks, the manifestations of my mother's presence continued. One vivid memory stands out. When I used to leave home to pick up my daughter from school, I would habitually call my mom. We'd have these conversations where I could share anything, and she would listen patiently. As she became ill, these calls became less frequent, and I felt a void growing. Someone later asked me, "Who filled that role for you as your mom began to decline?" My answer was Alain Cardon. In the same measure that the depth of conversations with my mom diminished due to her illness, my connection with Alain deepened. The conversations with him became a source of wisdom and comfort, filling the gap my mother's absence created.

Two ladies, Shelle and Geanina, also stepped into my life with maternal energy and guidance. It felt as though my mom had orchestrated a transition, ensuring her presence and love would persist through others.

I didn't cry at Mom's funeral. Instead, I felt a sense of profound peace. I understood that my mother had not left but transformed, and her presence scattered like seeds into the world around me. The law of transformation revealed its truth: nothing is lost, all is transformed. My mother continued to be with me—not just in my memories but in the people, the events, and the moments that carried her presence on.

The Gift of People Passing

When my mother passed away, one of the many thoughts that surfaced in my mind was, "I can finally do x, y, and z." For instance, if she were still alive, I wouldn't feel as free to speak openly about my relationship with her or the circumstances and experiences I've been through.

The incredible gift my mother gave me with her passing is the freedom to share my story—my truth—without causing her any pain in her physical form. I truly believe that where she is now, and in the relationship we have today, she is at peace with my openness.

If she had continued to live, I know it would have been difficult, if not impossible, for me to talk about certain aspects of our relationship—the hurts and pains that shaped it. Her passing allowed me to speak my truth in a new way.

When someone passes away, they leave behind an extraordinary gift through their departure. I often ask my clients, "What is the gift this human being has given you through their leaving? And when will you pick it up and use it?" This is how you truly honor them and their passing—by recognizing and embracing the unique gift they've left for you.

Transformation Is Not a Mental Process

My mom passed away on a Saturday morning. Just 2 days later, on Monday, I was scheduled to deliver a workshop for a company run by a good friend of mine, Diana. Diana was the executive director at the time, and when I informed her about my mom's passing on Saturday, her immediate response was, "Let's not do the workshop anymore." But I told her that we could go ahead with it and assured her that I was fine.

I vividly remember how I felt at that time. There was no pain in my heart—I was genuinely at peace. I had experienced a profound transformation. I delivered the workshop on Monday without any issues. People were curious and even amazed. They asked me, "How is it that you're doing so well? You're so luminous. Can I give you a hug?" I just smiled and said "I really am okay." And I truly was, because I had seen the transformation and understood the bigger picture.

Being present with my mom during her final moments was one of the most powerful spiritual experiences of my life. What I felt in that moment was extraordinary—something beyond words, almost like it belonged to the realm of science fiction. I was able to feel my mom's presence in such a profound way. It was sunrise in Transylvania when she passed away, a time when life was reawakening. It was also spring. April in Transylvania is magical—everything is blooming, flowers adorn the apple trees, and life seems to emerge wherever you look. My mom's passing coincided with this vibrant burst of life.

I decided to walk to the workshop on that Monday morning. For 30 minutes, I strolled through this explosion of spring— brilliant blue skies, flowers blooming, birds chirping, the crisp morning air reviving my lungs. I could feel my mom with me. She loved flowers and often sent me pictures of them. Her phone was filled with these images—moments where she captured the beauty that she so cherished. As I walked to the workshop venue, I paused to admire the radiant blossoms on the trees and even found myself snapping pictures of them. Her presence was there again.

The transformation I experienced after my mom's passing was not a mental process. It wasn't something I rational- ized or worked through intellectually. If it had been purely mental, I wouldn't have been able to run a workshop just 2 days later or experience such a profound sense of peace and alignment. That kind of transformation doesn't happen on a rational level.

There are principles and universal laws that guide us in tran- sitioning from a purely mental, rational process to one that transforms our entire being. When transformation reaches the physical level, it signifies that the work is complete. If the process remains confined to the mental level, the best outcome is mere acceptance. And while acceptance is sig- nificant, it's only 90% of the journey. The most critical step is the final one—the one that takes you to 100% completion. That's the step where true love and alignment reside.

For me, this wasn't about acceptance. It was about embodying the transformation and experiencing it in every aspect of my being. That's why I could move forward with clarity and lightness, seeing my mom's presence around me.

Definition of the Law of Transformation

The law of transformation says that

nothing is lost, everything transforms.

It stems from the conservation laws of physics[41] that can be summarized with the famous first law of thermodynamics articulated in the 1850s: "Energy can neither be created nor destroyed, only transformed from one form to another."[42]

Imagine a swinging pendulum. When the pendulum is at its highest point, it has maximum potential energy (stored due to its height). As it swings down, that potential energy turns into kinetic energy (energy of motion). At the lowest point, the pendulum has maximum kinetic energy and almost no potential energy. As it swings back up, the kinetic energy transforms back into potential energy.

---

41 The conservation laws of physics are fundamental principles stating that certain quantities in an isolated system remain constant over time, regardless of the processes occurring within the system. These laws are foundational to understanding the behavior of physical systems and include: conservation of energy, conservation of linear momentum, conservation of angular momentum, conservation of mass, conservation of electric charge, conservation of baryon number, conservation of lepton number, conservation of information.

42 The phrasing of this law varies slightly across sources, but is widely attributed to Rudolf Clausius and William Thomson (Lord Kelvin) during the formulation of the first law of thermodynamics in the 1850s. See, for example, Peter Atkins, *Four Laws That Drive the Universe* (Oxford University Press, 2007), 12.

Throughout the swing, the total energy (potential + kinetic) remains constant.

Antoine Lavoisier, known as the "father of modern chemistry," conducted meticulous experiments to measure mass before and after chemical reactions in the 1770s and 1780s. His experiments demonstrated that matter is neither created nor destroyed in chemical reactions, but merely changes form. He published his conclusion in 1789, saying that "in every operation, there is an equal quantity of matter before and after the operation."[43] This was later incorporated into the broader conservation of mass-energy in Einstein's theory of relativity.

Alchemists have studied the law of transformation for thousands of years, exploring the mysteries of change and evolution. In the last 300 years, modern science has expanded upon some of their ancient insights, delving deeper into the nature of transformation. Yet despite our progress, there is still so much we don't understand. For instance, science has yet to provide a definitive explanation of what energy truly is.[44] We can observe its effects, measure its impact, and harness its power, yet its fundamental nature remains elusive. In many ways, we are still at the very beginning of understanding the profound law of transformation.

More than 2500 years ago, Heraclitus said that the only constant in life is change, because "everything flows" (*panta*

---

43 Antoine Lavoisier, *Traité élémentaire de chimie* [*Elementary Treatise on Chemistry*] (Cuchet, 1789).

44 Energy is one of the most fundamental concepts in physics, but it is defined operationally, not ontologically. That means science describes what energy does (e.g., its conservation, transfer, measurement) rather than what it "is" in essence. Famous physicists, including Richard Feynman, have acknowledged this. In The Feynman Lectures on Physics, he said: "It is important to realize that in physics today, we have no knowledge of what energy is."

rhei).[45] There is nothing permanent about this world, except change. In Heraclitus's philosophy, change arises from the law of duality, meaning that opposites are not in contradiction, but are deeply interconnected and give rise to one another. For Heraclitus, opposites like day and night, life and death, or peace and war are not separate entities but part of the same reality.

Change occurs because these opposites are in constant tension, and it is this dynamic tension that drives the transformation of things. For example, health is understood in relation to sickness, and rest is meaningful only because of motion. Heraclitus uses the metaphor of a river to illustrate this: the river remains the same (unity) even though its waters (pairs of opposites) are always flowing and changing. This perpetual flux is the essence of existence, where opposites are working together in the ongoing process of transformation.

The One and the Many

A client who attended our Power on Heels program 3 years ago was in her mid-30s and claimed she couldn't find the right relationship. She was beautiful, fit, healthy, and earning significantly more than average. Her situation intrigued me. How could someone like her—a high earner with strong professional ethics, beauty, and health—not have a long line of qualified partners eager to be with her?

During the program, I guided her through an exercise to uncover the qualities she wanted in a partner. I asked, "What

---

45 Heraclitus, Fragment DK B91, quoted in Plato, *Cratylus* 402a. Translation adapted from T. M. Robinson, *Heraclitus: Fragments* (University of Toronto Press, 1987), 53.

do you really want from a man? What are the key traits you value most?" She listed the top 5 qualities she was looking for. "Intelligent conversations" was first on her list.

I then asked, "Who in your life offers you intelligent conversations?" Without hesitation, she replied, "My father, my friend Sam, my business partner Michael, and my sister Joanne."

"Beautiful! You've spread the qualities you want across multiple people instead of seeking them all in one individual. Can you see it?" She was taken aback, and I continued, "This happens because you associate more pain than pleasure with having the traits in one individual. Past hurt makes you believe it's safer to spread those traits across various relationships rather than risk disappointment with one." She nodded, reflecting on the insight.

She completed the protocol and by the end of the program, she had a renewed perspective on love and relationships. Six months later, she sent us a message saying she had found her "Prince Charming." Within 2 years, they were married and had started a beautiful family together.

In this case, the law of transformation works much like a bank. If you go to a bank and ask for a $250,000 loan, the bank will require collateral. If you can't provide it, you won't get the loan. It's that simple. But if you can offer collateral, you're likely to receive the loan. Sometimes that collateral comes from a friend, and that's perfectly acceptable to the bank—it still represents your value.

Similarly, when you want to manifest the relationship of your dreams, you must already acknowledge what you seek as being present in your life. If you fail to see those traits already existing, the "bank of life" withholds them. But when you recognize that the traits you desire in a partner are already there in different forms, "the bank" grants you what you're asking for.

Moving from Many to One and from One to Many

We've all experienced a phase in life where we were searching for a relationship. During this phase, it's natural to interact with multiple people, evaluating who aligns with our preferences and dismissing those who don't. We initially explore with several potential partners, even if some of them exist only in our mind. Over time, we make a choice and commit to one individual, transitioning from many possibilities to one single focus. Ideally, this choice brings fulfillment, and the relationship moves forward.

After committing to one, however, we notice more potential partners. Sometimes, individuals who weren't available during our search suddenly appear, presenting new options. This can lead to feelings of guilt, as we might believe that being committed means we shouldn't notice or be interested in others. But this guilt stems from a misunderstanding of the law of the one and the many.

The law of the one and the many is how Plotinus[46] named the law of duality in the 3rd century CE. The law of transformation is a byproduct of the law of duality, as Heraclitus wrote. Therefore the name "the law of the one and the many" can refer both to the law of duality *and* the law of transformation.

---

46 Plotinus, the founder of Neoplatonism, addresses the concept of "the one and the many" in his major work, the *Enneads*. His writings deeply explore the relationship between unity (the One) and multiplicity (the Many).

THE 7 UNIVERSAL LAWS

Searching for a job is similar to searching for a mate. First, we explore a few alternatives. Sometimes none of them feel right, so we keep searching. Other times, we wait because we don't like any of the available options. Eventually we come across a position that looks interesting enough and decide to accept the offer. Yet after starting the job, we might notice other opportunities. In the ensuing days and weeks, new and potentially better options may emerge on your horizon. Some people get confused and have all kinds of questions in their mind: "Did I make the right choice?" "What if the other option was better?" "Why do I have these thoughts?".

In both examples, these patterns illustrate how the mind naturally moves from many to one and then back to many. This is the law of transformation in action. There's nothing inherently wrong or unnatural about it. You don't need to have second thoughts about your choice or feel guilty for noticing new possibilities after making a commitment. This is simply a reflection of a universal principle at work.

The Law of Transformation in Business

I remember a client, Olivia, who participated in our Inspired Money program 4 years ago. She used to describe herself as having always been poor, with no wealth. She grew up in modest conditions in a small town with parents who could not offer her financial support.

When she started the program with us, she was functioning at what I call the "survival level." She was the CEO of a non-profit organization—which, statistically speaking, are not prosperous environments—and was constantly struggling for resources and funding. She felt like she was living month to month, as she struggled to secure the next source of funding for her organization, and there were times she couldn't even pay herself a full salary.

No matter what she did, she couldn't break out of this survival level. During that time, she had wealth in the form of travel, and she traveled extensively through her work. She also had wealth in the form of networking, as she had many relationships and friends all over the world. But she did not have wealth in the form of money.

Every month, as CEO, she worried about how she would pay salaries. Every month, she wondered what kind of sponsorships she could secure and questioned whether she would be able to get a full salary. Every month, she feared she wouldn't be able to afford her next trip.

In the Inspired Money program, clients complete an exercise in which they identify the forms of wealth they've experienced throughout their lives. They reflect on different life stages—such as preschool, kindergarten, elementary school, middle school, high school, university, up to age 30, then up to age 40, and so on. We use the law of transformation to assist clients in seeing how wealth showed up for them based on what truly mattered during each stage.

If you perceive something as missing in your life today, it creates a sense of void—and you can't create from a place of lack. But if you can recognize the form in which wealth appeared at each stage, you'll see how prosperity has transformed in your life over time.

This universal law helps reveal how each form of wealth served you. Every transformation happens for your benefit.

According to the law of transformation, you manifest what you need in the form that best supports you and your mission. Over the years, you've attracted wealth in the forms that were most aligned with your needs at the time.

For instance, in the early years of your life, perhaps your family was the wealth you had—the people close to you, your parents, grandparents, siblings, the house, and the yard you played in—all of which were an entire world for you. Remember when we were kids and every little shiny object felt like a hidden treasure? These small things, meaningless to adults, fascinated us. That was the form in which some people experienced wealth.

Later, when you went to kindergarten, wealth came in other forms. Perhaps you had a teacher who provided wealth in the form of knowledge and affection. You had many toys, playdough, colored pencils, and other things you loved but didn't have at home. Wealth was in a different form at that age. And as you grew, wealth transformed into various other forms.

When Olivia realized that throughout her life she had always experienced wealth in the form she needed most at the time, something shifted in her mind—she began to see herself as wealthy. She saw that wealth had always been present and was never absent from her life. She understood that wealth wasn't somewhere else, separate from her—it had always been with her.

At the end of the Inspired Money program, Olivia secured the largest funding her organization had ever received. This funding lifted the organization out of that month-to-month survival mode and provided peace of mind with a longer-term project. If I remember correctly, the funding ensured the organization's financial stability for a year.

Then, 2 years later, Olivia resigned from her position at the organization and accepted a job offer with a salary 5 times higher. This new role was in a non-profit organization that did not face financial issues and had consistent supporters.

The law of transformation helped Olivia to see how wealth had manifested in various forms throughout different stages of her life, from family and relationships to knowledge and travel. By recognizing these different forms of wealth, she shifted her mindset from focusing on what she lacked to acknowledging the abundance she had always had. This transformed her perception of her financial situation and opened the door to new opportunities, like securing funding and ultimately landing a higher-paying job.

Questions for Applying the Law of Transformation

Here is a summary of the questions we use in applying the law of transformation. You've already noticed them in the stories described in this chapter, but it might help to see them in one place.

- What do you perceive you've lost?
- What is the new form in which it has appeared in your life?
- What were the drawbacks of the old form?
- What benefits do you get from its new form?

Often, we choose to combine the law of transformation with the law of synchronicity (see chapter 6) for greater efficiency. For example:

- What do you perceive you have lost?
- What did you gain at exactly the same time?

The principle of quantitative and qualitative compensation applies here as well. You'll need to find a higher number of responses to achieve quantitative compensation for draw-backs and benefits, and have a few truly meaningful ones to achieve qualitative depth.

I travel with my husband most of the time. But occasionally he travels alone to attend courses or meet with other entre-preneurs, and we find ourselves thousands of kilometers apart. When we talk on the phone, he often asks me, "Who has picked up my traits? Who has taken up my behaviors?" We have fun with these questions. Sometimes, though, I don't want to see it because I prefer his form—I want *him* to take care of me, to cuddle me, to tell me nice things. So I resist and pretend that the law of transformation doesn't exist.

I recently went on a hike with my daughter and 2 dear friends. My husband stayed home because he chose to work. The hike was special—we climbed a mountain during the night to catch the sunrise at the summit, and we had a guide who took us there. The guide took care of me, holding my hand during some of the more challenging parts of the hike. It reminded me so much of what Stefan usually does—he holds my hand when we walk or hike together. It was amusing and heartwarming to notice his presence this way—although he was at home, he was present with me.

The more we ask these questions, the more attuned we become to life's hidden order. It takes practice and honesty, especially when the new form doesn't come in the shape we prefer. But with each realization, our resistance softens, and transformation becomes not just bearable, but beautiful.

3 Key Principles of the Law of Transformation

I'd like to share 3 principles related to the law of transformation that we work with day by day in our practice.

Principle 1: You Have Everything You Need in the Exact Form You Need It—Nothing Is Missing

This principle is fundamental when we apply the law of transformation. It suggests that everything in your life exists in the form that best serves your growth and purpose at any given moment. For example, if I have a romantic partner in a specific form and we break up, it doesn't mean that the essence of the partnership disappears. Instead, the energy of that connection transforms into the form that best serves me moving forward.

This concept applies to all relationships. When my mom passed away, she didn't vanish from my life. Her presence continues to exist in the exact form that I need for my path and mission. How do we determine the right form? It's the form that serves our journey most efficiently and effectively.

Principle 2: Every Individual Possesses All Traits.

This second principle of the law of transformation is closely related to the law of reflection. When it comes to traits, you don't lose or gain them. Instead, traits transform over time. You possess all traits inherently, and by applying the law of transformation you can shift the form of the traits to achieve your goals. This principle implies a profound truth: traits are conserved, much like the conservation law of energy in the universe or the conservation law of information.

This understanding also challenges certain idealized perceptions. For instance, if you believe in figures who are all-positive, all-enlightened, or devoid of any negativity, this principle suggests that such states would violate the conservation of energy and conservation of information. Every individual embodies all aspects, both positive and negative, in a balanced and transformative way.

Another implication is that your familial traits remain with you constantly, although in different forms. Your mother's energy, for instance, will manifest in different ways through various people or experiences. The same applies to fathers, siblings, and even children. You'll always find these dynamics present, expressed through different relationships and interactions. Similarly, you'll take on the roles of parent, sibling, or child for others—regardless of biological ties.

Principle 3: When a Relationship or Situation No Longer Serves Your Mission, Transformation Becomes Inevitable

The third crucial principle addresses struggles and conflicts. Struggles often arise when we resist transformation. Whether it's a friendship, marriage, romantic relationship, or business partnership, when the form of that connection ceases to serve you, transformation is required. If you don't initiate the transformation proactively, struggles and conflicts will force it upon you.

For example, consider a romantic relationship. Relationships evolve as individuals grow, and maintaining outdated dynamics will lead to tension. When the "operating system" of a relationship becomes misaligned with the individuals' growth, conflict emerges.

This misalignment might show up as an affair or a sudden desire to leave. For example, one might find a new job opportunity elsewhere and insist on wanting to take that opportunity and leave. These situations signal the need to upgrade the relationship's "operating system" to reflect the current realities of both individuals. This dynamic isn't limited to romantic relationships—it's equally true for friendships, business collaborations, and other partnerships.

In summary, the law of transformation encompasses 3 vital principles:

- You have everything you need in the exact form you need it. Nothing is missing.
- Every individual possesses all traits.
- Transformation is inevitable when a form no longer serves you.

Understanding and applying these principles allows you to navigate life's changes with greater awareness and intention, embracing transformation as a natural and beneficial process.

Where You Can Apply the Law of Transformation

The law of transformation can be applied across various areas of life to help navigate change and loss, and manifest desired outcomes. Here are some of the most common scenarios where this powerful law can be used:

1. Dealing with Loss

One of the most frequent applications of the law of transformation arises when we experience the departure of someone from our lives. This could include the passing of a loved one, a child leaving for college, or the end of a relationship.

The loss of a pet can also be profound. For example, I worked with my friend and client, Bianca, when her beloved dog passed away. This pet was like a child to her. In the past, similar losses had caused her to grieve for months. After we worked together for 2 consecutive sessions, however, Bianca found peace and calm. She was able to achieve emotional balance within 2 days instead of 2 months.

2. Inviting the Right Partner into Your Life

The law of transformation can be intentionally applied to create a fulfilling relationship. We use a structured protocol to support this goal, including steps to address and balance the pain associated with relationships.

The principle is simple: if you associate more pain than pleasure with the idea of a relationship, you're unlikely to manifest one successfully. By transforming and rebalancing this inner dynamic, you align yourself to attract the partner you truly desire.

3. Improving Your Relationship with Money

Similar transformative processes are used to shift your relationship with money. These techniques are often incorporated into our advanced courses, enabling participants to break through financial blocks and align themselves with abundance.

4. Coping with Physical Loss or Changes

Physical changes or losses—such as an accident leading to the loss of a limb, hair loss, or reduced skin elasticity—can also be addressed using the law of transformation. Even challenges like gaining weight can benefit from this approach. By transforming your perceptions, you can find a new level of inner order and self-mastery in the face of these changes.

5. Navigating Financial and Business-Related Losses

The law of transformation plays a significant role in our Inspired Money program. A chapter in this program addresses financial losses, such as loss of money, losing an employee, or loss of products and other assets.

In these situations, the law of transformation helps balance the perceived loss and brings peace of mind. Combined with the law of duality and other principles, the law of transformation enables you to recognize that what you have lost now exists in a different, more efficient form for your life's alignment.

The Universal Perspective

A key aspect of the law of transformation is the understanding that there are no mistakes in the universe. If something leaves your life, it is aligned with your soul's journey and the divine plan. This law helps you perceive the new form in which your perceived loss has manifested, and reach a state of gratitude and love for the new form. This perspective not only brings peace, but also empowers you to move forward with clarity and purpose.

In summary, the law of transformation is a versatile and profound tool that can bring balance, clarity, and power to various areas of life. Whether it's coping with loss, manifesting relationships, or navigating significant changes, this law helps you align with the energy of life.

Practical Application

Now that you've explored the core ideas of this chapter, it's time to put them into action.

1. Transform the Perception of Loss

Pick something you perceive you've lost recently. Ideally, choose something that doesn't carry intense emotions, for the purpose of this exercise.

Now, ask yourself the following questions:

- What do you perceive you've lost?
- What is the meaning you gave it?

For instance, someone lost a sum of money and the meaning is that they lost their safety net. Another example is losing an employee and the meaning is that the business lost 25% of their capacity to serve the clients.

Next, ask:

- What is the new form in which it has appeared in your life? It can have multiple forms.
- What benefits do you get from its new form? Find at least 25 benefits.

- What were the drawbacks of the old form? Find at least 25 drawbacks.

In the end, ask yourself the verification question: Do you perceive that the new form has equal benefits to the old form? If they are equal, you've completed the exercise. If not, continue identifying more drawbacks and benefits.

2. Create the Love You Truly Want

If one of your top goals is to find the right partner to share your life with, we can support you more effectively than traditional coaching or therapy, as you've seen through some of the stories in this chapter.

Many people lose hope after repeated disappointments in relationships. But no matter what you've been through, a fulfilling relationship is still possible. Book a call with one of our consultants using the link below, and we'll connect you with an FTP specialist who can assist you. It could save you years of unnecessary struggle.

InspiredLifeCircle.com/book-call-7

3. Overcoming a Financial Plateau

One of the main reasons people reach a financial plateau is the losses they've experienced. In our language, these losses are translated as unfair exchanges: when you received less than you believed you deserved or when something was taken from you. These are perceptions that violate the law of transformation, which is why they hurt. In essence, you block your business or financial growth by refusing to experience more of that type of pain.

If you feel like you've hit a financial ceiling and nothing you do seems to move the needle, consider joining our Inspired Money program. This program is a transformative 9-week journey designed to support individuals break through financial limitations and develop a healthier relationship with money—better than ever before. It addresses the deep-rooted subconscious patterns that affect financial results and self-worth, ultimately enabling participants to expand their earning potential and financial confidence. Many people unlocked the next chapter of their financial journey during the program or shortly after, and you can view their experiences on our website. Apply now for a conversation with a program consultant at

InspiredLifeCircle.com/inspired-money

CHAPTER 6

THE LAW OF SYNCHRONICITY

All philosophers, of every school, imagine that causation is one of the fundamental axioms or postulates of science, yet, oddly enough, in advanced sciences such as gravitational astronomy, the word "cause" never occurs. [. . .] The law of causality, I believe, like much that passes muster among philosophers, is a relic of a bygone age, surviving, like the monarchy, only because it is erroneously supposed to do no harm.

— Bertrand Russell[47]

---

47 Bertrand Russell, "On the Notion of Cause," *Proceedings of the Aristotelian Society* 13 (1912): 1–2.

An Imaginary Experiment

Two advanced laboratories—Lab A in Paris and Lab B in Tokyo—are collaborating on a groundbreaking experiment. They have been provided with a pair of *entangled electrons*, created simultaneously in a special quantum generator. These electrons are linked in such a way that their quantum states are perfectly correlated.

Lab A has Electron A, and Lab B has Electron B. The electrons are now thousands of kilometers apart. Each team agrees to measure a property of their electron, such as spin (a quantum property). Spin can be measured as up or down along a chosen axis.

The Paris team decides to measure Electron A's spin along the vertical axis. Their instruments immediately report: *spin up*. At the same time as Lab A's measurement was done, the Tokyo team finds that Electron B's spin is *spin down*, even though they haven't communicated with Lab A.

This result isn't random—it always happens this way. If one lab measures *spin up*, the other lab observes *spin down*, and vice versa.

The Paris and Tokyo teams scratch their heads. How can the measurement in Paris instantaneously reveal the result in Tokyo, thousands of kilometers away?

You will see in this chapter how these ideas evolved in the last 100 years.

Definition of the Law of Synchronicity

The law of synchronicity states that

in every perceived moment there is an equal amount of support and challenge.

This applies to other pairs of complementary opposites— like benefits and drawbacks, pain and pleasure—whether we see them or not. If we perceive one side, the other is present too, at the exact synchronous moment.

The law of synchronicity is the law of duality applied to each moment. One could say it is the law of duality at its finest— brought to a very concrete level, in every instant.

The logic is straightforward: if there is a constant balance, as discussed in chapter 1 on the law of duality, then that balance must be present in every moment. Otherwise, it would imply that overall there is God's order, but in this particular moment there is none—and that's not possible.

As I presented in chapter 3, maximum growth occurs at the border of support and challenge. That's where your greatest capacity for growth lies and you're capable of extraordinary things. When you're aligned—or "on your path"—you embrace both challenge and support equally. If you're not on your path, you'll give up when faced with a challenge. This distinction is essential.

Now let's bring this concept into the moment. In every moment, you experience both support and challenge—and you have 2 choices. If you recognize them as present simultaneously and embrace them both, you bring out the best in yourself. If you see support and challenge as separate, it means you're not aligned with that path. The pain becomes a signal, urging you to move forward and seek challenges where you can handle the discomfort. It's a feedback mechanism guiding you toward a path where you can embrace both pain and pleasure at once.

Among all the 7 universal laws I work with, the law of synchronicity is the most difficult to apply, and it requires skill and experience. To perceive synchronicity, you must be fully present in the moment. There's no other way. It can't be applied intellectually alone. It's like meditating—you need to close your eyes, disconnect from the outside world, and fully connect yourself with the moment you're working with.

Unfortunately, people's minds are increasingly scattered and less present. It takes a great deal of clarification for clients to grasp, which is why I work less frequently with the law of synchronicity. But when I do, it creates miracles—like in Jung's story with the scarab and his client, which you'll read about later in this chapter.

Another reason the law of synchronicity is so challenging to apply is that it represents a completely different paradigm— the opposite of the cause-and-effect thinking we're so accustomed to. The concept of acausality is nearly impossible to fully grasp, which is part of what makes quantum physics so difficult to understand. This law mirrors the principles of quantum mechanics, making it just as elusive for the linear mind to comprehend.

How Einstein and Bohr's Debate Led to a Quantum Revolution

The 1920s were the early days of quantum physics, when scientists found themselves staring into an abyss of uncertainty. The microscopic world they were discovering seemed to defy everything they thought they knew about reality. At the center of this scientific revolution stood 2 titans of physics: Albert Einstein, whose theories had already reshaped our understanding of the universe, and the Danish physicist Niels Bohr, who was pioneering the emerging field of quantum mechanics.

The story begins with Bohr making a declaration that would shake the foundations of physics: he claimed that subatomic particles don't have specific, fixed properties until they are observed. Before a particle is observed, it exists in a state of many possibilities (a superposition). The act of observing the particle forces it to "choose" one of those possibilities, making that specific outcome part of our reality. This idea was more than just strange—it threatened to upend centuries of scientific thinking about the nature of reality itself.

Einstein, despite his crucial role in laying the groundwork for quantum theory, found himself increasingly troubled by its implications. The conflict came to a head in 1935, when Einstein and his colleagues, Boris Podolsky and Nathan Rosen, published a paper that would become famous in the history of physics. Their argument centered on a peculiar quantum phenomenon that seemed impossible: pairs of particles that remained mysteriously connected no matter how far apart they were.[48]

Einstein and his team argued that this was absurd. How could 2 particles possibly coordinate their properties instantaneously across vast distances? Such communi-

---

[48] Albert Einstein, Boris Podolsky, & Nathan Rosen, "Can Quantum-Mechanical Description of Physical Reality Be Considered Complete?" *Physical Review*, 47, no. 10 (1935), 777 780.

cation would need to travel faster than light—something Einstein's theory of relativity had proven impossible.

Einstein famously dismissed this apparent connection between particles as "spooky action at a distance."[49] He was convinced that quantum mechanics must be incomplete, missing some hidden variables that would explain everything rationally. Bohr, however, remained unruffled. He argued that Einstein's mistake was thinking of the particles as separate entities in the first place. In Bohr's view, they were part of an indivisible whole, and their apparent separation was an illusion. Just as Heraclitus, almost 2500 years ago, Bohr was thinking about the unity of opposites, and he viewed opposites as being one and the same.[50]

For decades, this debate remained largely theoretical. But science has a way of demanding evidence, and in 1964 physicist John Bell devised a mathematical framework to test these ideas.[51] The real breakthrough came in the early 1980s, when French physicist Alain Aspect and his team conducted groundbreaking experiments with pairs of entangled photons. Their results showed something remarkable: the particles really did seem to be instantaneously connected, just as quantum mechanics had predicted.[52]

---

49 Albert Einstein to Max Born, 3 March 1947, in *The Born-Einstein Letters: Correspondence between Albert Einstein and Max and Hedwig Born, 1916–1955*, ed. by Irene Born (Walker, 1971), 158.

50 Niels Bohr, "Can Quantum-Mechanical Description of Physical Reality Be Considered Complete?" *Physical Review* 48, no. 8 (1935): 696–702.

51 John S. Bell, "On the Einstein Podolsky Rosen Paradox," *Physics Physique Физика* 1, no. 3 (1964): 195–200.

52 Alain Aspect, Jean Dalibard, and Gérard Roger, "Experimental Test of Bell's Inequalities Using Time-Varying Analyzers," Physical Review Letters 49, no. 25 (1982): 1804–1807.

The final confirmation came in 2015, when scientists conducted what they called a "loophole-free" test, addressing all possible alternative explanations. The results were clear: quantum entanglement was real. Particles really could be connected in ways that seemed to transcend space and time.[53]

What Einstein had dismissed as "spooky" turned out to be one of the most profound discoveries in physics. Today, quantum entanglement isn't just a curiosity—it's the foundation for revolutionary technologies like quantum computing. The debate between Einstein and Bohr, which began as a philosophical disagreement about the nature of reality, has evolved into one of the most promising frontiers of modern science.

In the end, both Einstein and Bohr contributed to our understanding of this mysterious quantum dance. Einstein's skepticism pushed scientists to rigorously test quantum theory, while Bohr's intuition about the interconnected nature of reality pointed the way toward discoveries that continue to astonish us today. Their intellectual duel helped unveil a universe more mysterious and interconnected than anyone had imagined—a universe where particles can remain eternally entangled in their quantum dance, regardless of the space between them.

---

53 Bas Hensen et al., "Loophole-Free Bell Inequality Violation Using Electron Spins Separated by 1.3 Kilometres," *Nature* 526, no. 7575 (2015): 682–686.

Lynden K. Shalm et al., "Strong Loophole-Free Test of Local Realism," *Physical Review Letters* 115, no. 25 (2015): 250402.

Marissa Giustina et al., "Significant-Loophole-Free Test of Bell's Theorem with Entangled Photons," *Physical Review Letters* 115, no. 25 (2015): 250401.

Jung's Synchronicity: An Acausal Connecting Principle

About the same time as the physicists were discovering synchronicity in quantum mechanics, another great mind, Carl Gustav Jung (1875-1961), started to talk about it in the realm of psychology. The Swiss psychiatrist and psychotherapist started considering synchronicity as a concept in the 1920s and he publicly shared in his lectures and developed it further in the 1930s to the 1950s. Jung's belief was that, just as events may be connected by causality, they may also be connected acausally, by meaning (entanglement).

Jung had been pondering the phenomenon of synchronicity for decades before publishing his book in 1952, *Synchronicity: An Acausal Connecting Principle*, with the Nobel-prize-winning physicist Wolfgang Pauli.

Jung and Pauli jointly developed the concept of synchronicity—events that are acausally connected but experienced as meaningfully linked based on the observer's subjective context, bridging internal and external realities. They also found a shared analogy between the atom with its nucleus and orbiting electrons, and the self—comprising a central conscious ego surrounded by the unconscious.

Jung's first source of inspiration for discovering synchronicity was his work with patients. In his clinical practice, Jung encountered numerous instances where patients reported meaningful coincidences that had profound psychological significance. One famous example is the story of the golden scarab.

In the early days of his psychiatric practice in Zürich, Dr. Jung faced a particularly challenging case. His patient was a highly educated woman whose strong rational mindset and Cartesian philosophy had proven resistant to therapy. Three doctors had tried and failed to help her before she sat in Jung's office, her intellectual armor seemingly impenetrable.

During one pivotal session, as the morning light filtered through Jung's office window, the woman began describing a dream she'd had the previous night. In it, she had been given a golden scarab—a precious object that held deep significance in ancient Egyptian mythology as a symbol of rebirth and transformation.

As she spoke, Jung noticed something peculiar. A gentle tapping sound came from behind him, where his office window faced the lake. The noise grew more persistent, catching both their attention. When Jung turned to investigate, he was astonished to see a small beetle repeatedly striking the glass, trying to enter the darkened room—behavior quite unusual for its species.

Rising from his chair, Jung opened the window and caught the insect in mid-flight. To his amazement, it was a scarab beetle, with a golden-green coloring that made it the closest possible match to the golden scarab from his patient's dream. This species was rarely seen in that climate, and its appearance at that precise moment seemed to defy ordinary explanation.

The effect on his patient was profound. The rational fortress she had built around herself began to crack. The sheer improbability of this coincidence—describing a dream about a golden scarab while a similar beetle appeared in reality—challenged her purely logical worldview. This synchronistic event became the breakthrough Jung had been seeking, allowing the therapeutic process to finally move forward.

This incident not only transformed the course of his patient's therapy, but also became one of the cornerstone examples in Jung's development of his theory of synchronicity—meaningful coincidences that couldn't be explained by simple cause and effect. As Jung would later note, this was the only time in his entire career that such a beetle appeared at his window, making the coincidence even more remarkable.[54]

When I first found out about this story I was blown away because this is exactly how I work—observing and appreciating these meaningful coincidences. I learned this type of work from one of my mentors, Alain Cardon, the founder of Systemic Coaching. I was amazed to see that Jung used similar methods 100 years ago.

Jung's second source of inspiration for exploring synchronicity was his relationship with the physicist Wolfgang Pauli (1900-1958), who was deeply interested in the intersection of physics and psychology.

Jung and Pauli first connected in the late 1920s, when Pauli was experiencing significant personal turmoil. His mother had recently died by suicide, and his first marriage had ended in divorce. Pauli sought psychological help and eventually became one of Jung's patients. This therapeutic relationship later evolved into a mutual intellectual exchange.

---

54 C. G. Jung, *Synchronicity: An Acausal Connecting Principle*, in *The Structure and Dynamics of the Psyche*, vol. 8 of The Collected Works of C. G. Jung, trans. R. F. C. Hull (Princeton University Press, 1970), §845.

The letters between Jung and Pauli, published in *Atom and Archetype: The Pauli/Jung Letters 1932-1958*, reveal the depth of their intellectual dialogue. These letters explore their shared fascination with the interplay between science, psychology, and spirituality.

Besides synchronicity, both men explored the idea of the *unus mundus*, Latin for "one world," a unified underlying reality where psyche and matter are not separate but inter-connected aspects of the same fundamental essence. And both of their ideas influenced the other's, helping each to refine their own theories and expertise.

Pauli's scientific perspective helped Jung refine his ideas about the relationship between psychology and the physical world, especially in the context of synchronicity. Jung cited Pauli's input in his writings on this topic, particularly in his book on synchronicity. Jung's psychological theories provided Pauli with a framework for considering the subjec-tive and intuitive dimensions of scientific discovery. Pauli's engagement with Jung may have influenced his thinking about complementarity and the philosophical implications of quantum mechanics.

First Question to Apply the Law of Synchronicity: *Who Did the Equal Opposite at the Exact Same Moment?*

This law can be effectively applied to emotional "wounds" such as abandonment, rejection, and humiliation. It works in all moments of life where you can identify the opposite actions or behaviors—and identifying those opposites can be done quite effectively by asking the questions you'll see in this chapter.

The "wound of abandonment" is a deep emotional pain that arises when an individual perceives they have been abandoned or left alone—whether physically or emotionally. This wound usually forms in childhood, often due to insecure relationships with parents or caregivers.

A person with the "wound of abandonment" might experience an intense fear of being left behind—as was my case—a constant fear that loved ones will leave. They might feel an excessive need for approval or attention and become jealous, possessive, or overly dependent on their partner. Sometimes a person with this specific wound might withdraw to avoid the risk of being abandoned again, tending to avoid deep connections for this reason.

In my situation, working on the "wound of abandonment" using the law of synchronicity was a memorable experience. I revisited every moment of my life which I had perceived as abandonment and asked, "Who did the equal opposite at this exact same moment? Who *chose* me in the exact moment I felt abandoned?"

I discovered that whenever I perceived abandonment by someone, another person chose me in that very same moment. The beauty was that when someone chose me, they usually valued me for who I truly was.

The most memorable moment I worked on was before birth. I wondered where this "wound of abandonment" might have originated, and realized it might have surfaced during my gestational period. I had learned that when my mother got pregnant with me, she became ill—she had some ovarian issues, and it was unclear what exactly was wrong. Her parents feared the worst. They wanted my mother to survive, and if necessary, to terminate the pregnancy. This was the standard thinking for parents at the time. It seems that, even though I was still in the womb, I could sense what was happening.

When I worked on this issue, I connected with the moment when my mother was pregnant and sick. I connected with that moment and felt the energy of my grandparents wanting to protect my mother while rejecting me.

I asked myself who had chosen me at the same time. The answer was overwhelming when it came. Being present in that moment, I saw that God had chosen me at the same time. Otherwise, I wouldn't have been born. It was a very powerful and enlightening moment.

I also worked on other moments when I felt abandoned, and managed to overcome this "wound of abandonment"— transforming it entirely by working only with the law of synchronicity. This is no small feat, but I no longer feel the intense fear of being abandoned. I have become much more free in my relationships with loved ones and am able to be truly present with them.

Normal and Extreme Circumstances

When I talk about the law of synchronicity or the law of duality, I often receive theoretical questions. These are usually scenarios imagined by the individual asking, and not events they have personally experienced. They present situations where they believe these laws might not apply, trying to reconcile them with their current paradigm.

I usually steer away from engaging in purely theoretical discussions because it's like trying to explain what it feels like to fall in love. Even if the person grasps the concept, it won't hold much significance until they've experienced it themselves. A friend of mine calls it "mental masturbation."

That being said, here are 2 common questions I receive, along with their answers. These are just examples to illustrate how these laws might apply in such scenarios.

Question #1

How does the law of synchronicity manifest when there are only 2 people involved? For example, if it's just Alex and Marta, and Marta criticizes Alex, who perceives that as a challenge. There is no one else present. How does the law come into play in this situation?

According to the principles outlined in the law of synchronicity, even in a situation where there are only 2 people physically present, the law still operates through the mental dynamics of the individuals involved.

In this scenario, when Marta criticizes Alex and he perceives it as a challenge, his mind will bring forth the presence of another individual—whether real or imagined—who demonstrates the opposite action toward him at that very moment. For example, in that exact moment when Alex perceives being criticised, someone else would be present with him in his mind, appreciating or praising him for the same quality Marta is criticizing, thereby creating the synchronicity.

The mind will always maintain balance. Thus, even if only Alex and Marta are physically present, the law of synchronicity ensures that the opposites are manifested through Alex's perception every second.

One important distinction: We don't use memory or imagination here, because they create space and time in the mind. Memory is about the past, imagination is about the future. When you are truly present, there is no time. So balance exists in the moment, in the timeless instant of pure presence, when eternity reveals itself to you. There, in presence, you see what you hadn't seen before—acausally. If you bring time into the equation, you create causality between answers, and it's no longer synchronicity.

Question #2

How does the law of synchronicity manifest in extremely challenging cases? For instance, if someone is being raped or tortured, and there is no one else around. The individual being raped or tortured is clearly experiencing challenge. Where is the support in this case?

A colleague of mine once shared a profound story about working with a client who had experienced trauma. The client had been raped when she was younger, and her memory of the event was dominated by feelings of being constrained and immobilized. During the session, the specialist working with her asked a striking question: "Where, at that exact same moment, did you feel free?" Initially, the client couldn't answer. The specialist then invited her to become fully present with the moment.

As she immersed herself in the moment, she saw that at the time of the trauma her mind created the opposite, placing her in a field of flowers and butterflies, a place where she felt completely free. Her mind, in the midst of the overwhelming constraint, had created this vivid image of freedom. The specialist assisted her to see that her mind had naturally maintained balance, holding both the challenge and its opposite—freedom and constraint—in the same moment. This realization brought the client a sense of relief, allowing her mind to become more flexible and begin its healing process.

The law of synchronicity is abundantly found in the stories of those martyred for their faith. Christian tradition, for instance, is rich with accounts of martyrs from the early centuries of the faith. These stories, often read in Christian churches, detail the agonies endured by martyrs, yet they also highlight moments of divine synchronicity.

Take the story of Saint Stephen, recognized in the Bible as the first Christian martyr. As described in Acts chapters 6 and 7, Stephen was arrested on false charges of blasphemy. Dragged outside the city, he faced a brutal death by stoning. Amidst the violence, something extraordinary occurred. Acts 7:55–56 recounts: "But Stephen, full of the Holy Spirit, looked up to heaven and saw the glory of God, and Jesus standing at the right hand of God. 'Look,' he said, 'I see heaven open.'"[55]

Even as Stephen's body was broken by the stones, his mind soared, entering a transcendent communion with God. This paradox of intense pain and divine bliss echoes throughout hundreds of stories of early Christian martyrs. It reveals a deeper truth: in the midst of our greatest suffering, there is a corresponding moment of profound spiritual or emotional connection—a manifestation of the universal law of synchronicity.

---

55 New International Version (NIV).

Both the story of the client and the accounts of Christian martyrs illustrate the mind's innate ability to maintain equilibrium, even in the most challenging circumstances.

Applying More Than One Law

Three years ago a new client, Diana, who ran a service-based business where she worked directly with clients, approached me. She struggled with a "wound of rejection." From time to time, she noticed that some clients preferred to work with her colleagues rather than with her, even if they initially started with her. Every time clients chose another colleague, she felt unappreciated, unwanted, and as though she wasn't good enough.

I remember the first time we met online, her hands tightly clasped together, a faint furrow between her brows. Diana came across as confident when we first met, but after the first minutes of the conversation, that confidence seemed to waver. The ease she initially exuded disappeared.

"I don't know what's wrong with me," she began, her voice tinged with uncertainty. "I started this business so I could help people, but sometimes, when clients choose to work with my colleagues instead of mc, I get really down." I nodded, encouraging her to continue.

"I know I shouldn't feel this way—my colleagues are talented, and I've trained them myself—but then envy creeps in. It's like I can't control it. And then I hate myself for feeling this way. I should be happy that my clients prefer to work with my colleagues—that's why I started the business, right?" But Diana's emotions didn't align with this logic, and she didn't know how to break free from these thoughts.

"Does it affect your relationships with your team?" I asked softly.

Her expression tightened. "It does," she admitted. "There was one colleague—she was amazing, and clients loved her. I fired her over a minor mistake—but the truth is, I couldn't handle how often she was chosen over me. I've never told anyone this before."

Diana's confession hung in the air. She shifted uncomfortably in her seat, her shoulders tense. I leaned forward slightly. "Diana, let's work on this. When a client doesn't choose you, what does that mean to you?"

She hesitated before answering, "It means I'm not valued enough for what I do."

"Alright," I said. "Now, go to a specific moment when a client didn't choose you. Are you there? Who was valuing you at that very moment?" She looked puzzled, her lips pressing together into a thin line. "What do you mean?"

"Go to a moment when a client didn't choose you," I said. "At that particular time, who valued you for your professional skills?" She fell silent, her brow knitting. Then slowly, she said, "My colleagues. They showed me their appreciation for how I run the business, manage clients, and even say no to clients when necessary."

"That's great," I said, nodding. "What else have they appreciated about you?"

Diana's eyes brightened a little, and she straightened in her seat as she began to list the ways they had shown their appreciation for her. "They've thanked me for teaching them how to set goals, stay focused, and maintain professional ethics. They've told me how much they've grown because of the support and training I've given them."

"Can you see the pattern here?" I asked.

She nodded slowly, though still unsure. "I think so, but what does it mean?"

"It's as if the universe is giving you a message," I explained. "Let's apply the law of fractals here. You know that recurring patterns in your life tend to show you where you need to focus. Think about it—every time a client chose someone else, did it seem like a sign?"

She blinked, processing the idea. "You mean, life was showing me that I needed to focus more on my business and on my team, rather than trying to be the go-to person for every client?"

"Right. It's an invitation to shift your focus—from working *in* your business to working *on* it. The more you build the structure of your business and strengthen your team, the more you grow as a leader."

Her eyes widened. "Wow," she said. "This has been happening over and over, and I've never looked at it that way."

"To go deeper," I continued, "let's use the law of duality. What benefits have you experienced from being chosen by your colleagues rather than your clients?"

Diana thought for a moment. "I've had more time to focus on strategy and work on strategic partnerships. And it's encouraged me to trust my team more."

"And what drawbacks might there have been if clients had chosen you every time?" I asked, anticipating the answer, which would truly shift her perspective.

"I'd have been too busy to focus on the bigger picture," she realized. "I would've burned out trying to do everything myself." Tears welled up in her eyes, and her expression shifted as the realization sank in.

"So, what does this mean for you now?" I asked. She exhaled, a slow, steady breath, and when she looked up again, there was light in her gaze.

"It means I don't have to resist it anymore," she said with a smile. "When clients choose my colleagues, it's not rejection—it's guidance to focus on my business and my team."

In the months that followed, Diana experienced the fruits of this shift in perspective. She stopped feeling down and sorry for herself whenever clients chose her colleagues over her. Because these feelings weren't sapping her energy anymore, she was able to pour her energy into building her business structure and strengthening her team. A year later, her business had doubled in size.

This session with Diana demonstrates how more than one universal law can be applied to a challenge someone wants to work on, coming together like different instruments in an orchestra to produce a beautiful result.

Applying Synchronicity on the Same Topic

In my work, the law of synchronicity is not always the most efficient to use—applying other universal laws will dissolve the charge faster and better. But other times, the law of synchronicity is without a doubt the most efficient.

For example, consider a situation where you're criticized, and it really hurts. To apply the law of synchronicity you will ask the question, *Who, at the same moment, did the equal opposite for you on the same issue?* But first, you must define the *opposite* in that moment. The opposite of criticism may be different from one moment to another, depending on the context. Let's say you'll define the opposite, in this case, as being praised for the same thing. Then, by seeing who praised you for it, you will see that your work is also valued, not just criticized. You see that appreciation is also there. And very quickly, your perspective on the situation becomes softer because you see both support and challenge.

For this to be effective, you need to find the opposite *on the same topic*. If someone says, "you're stupid, but you cook well," the two don't cancel each other out, because they are different topics. So make sure you look for the same topic when you work with the law of synchronicity.

A colleague of mine worked with a client, Gina, who carried a painful memory about her mother. "She criticized me in front of a bunch of other people when I was 17," Gina told her. "It was the first time I went out with a boy. I already felt so anxious about having my first boyfriend, and then she added to it. There was no need for her to do that." My colleague nodded, encouraging her to continue.

"It wasn't just the criticism," Gina explained. "There was more to it. I had told her something in secret, and then she shared it publicly. She betrayed my trust. I think she had 2 glasses of wine and just spoke without thinking."

"What happened after that?" my colleague asked.

Gina sighed. "I stopped trusting her. I decided I couldn't share anything with her anymore—at least, nothing that could make me vulnerable. I was hurt, and that wall between us has stayed up ever since. I'm 36 now, and I still don't trust her. Our conversations are mainly superficial. We don't connect anymore, not really."

My colleague leaned forward. "Let's work on this. Tell me, what would you have wanted from her at that moment?"

"I wanted her to be on my side," Gina said firmly.

My colleague paused. "Okay. Who was on your side at that very moment about the same topic of relationships?" Gina frowned, thinking hard. "No—no one."

"Let's take a different approach," my colleague suggested. "Close your eyes for a moment. Relax. I want you to go back to that moment—not thinking about it, but really feeling it. Be present with it. When you are truly present with the moment, and you are not intellectualizing it, the answer comes immediately. Who was on your side at that time, about relationships?"

Gina was quiet for a moment, her brow furrowed. Then her face softened. "At the table," she said slowly, "there was a 20-year-old boy. He was from the family we were visiting. At that age, 3 years older feels like a big deal, you know? He defended me. He understood me better than my mother did." Her voice grew lighter as she spoke. "He was on my side."

My colleague smiled. "That's the law of synchronicity at work. Even when it feels like no one is there for us, when we look closer, there's someone. Do you notice how realizing that changes the memory?"

Gina nodded. "It does. I don't feel so alone at that moment anymore."

My colleague let her sit with the realization for a moment before shifting to the next part of the story. "Now, about the secret your mother shared. Let's look at that. Who, at that same moment, did the opposite and kept your secrets?"

"My best friend at the time," Gina said immediately. But then her face fell. "It doesn't help much, though. It's like—that's not the part that really bothers me."

"Let's try something else," my colleague said. "Instead of focusing on who kept your secrets, let's look at your mother. Were there other secrets she kept for you—ones she didn't reveal?"

Gina's eyes widened. "Actually, yes," she said, almost surprised at her own realization. "There were several things I told her that she didn't share that day. I hadn't thought about that before."

"How does that change how you feel about her sharing that one secret?" my colleague asked.

Gina paused, reflecting deeply. "It makes it less painful. I see now that it wasn't a pattern of hers to betray me. She kept my trust in other ways." They sat in silence for a moment, letting it sink in.

Gina broke the silence. "It's like the criticism felt lighter when I realized someone else was on my side, and the weight of her telling my secret felt lighter when I saw all the other times she had kept my trust. It's not just about what happened—it's about what else was true at the same time."

"Exactly," my colleague said. "And you've done an incredible job of finding those moments."

By the end of their session, Gina's energy had shifted. The memory that had haunted her for nearly 2 decades no longer carried the same weight. She left with a new awareness and a balanced perspective on her relationship with her mother.

The Freedom in Recognizing We Lack Nothing

Several years ago, I worked with a client named Anna, a young woman with striking blue eyes that brimmed with emotion when she spoke. She harbored a great deal of resentment toward her father because she perceived that he had "never" supported her financially or emotionally. Whenever clients use absolute words like *all, everyone, never, always, every time, none,* or *nobody,* it's a sign that there's a strong emotional charge. In such situations, most clients need support because they can't balance their perspective on their own.

Anna's relationship with her father made her see men as adversaries. She also shared that she was stressed and struggling with anxiety, which was disrupting her sleep. It was clear that the resentment she harbored towards her dad was taking a toll on her well-being.

In our fourth session together, I invited her to apply the law of synchronicity: "Anna, please go to a moment when you perceive that your father did not support you financially and emotionally in your development."

"Well, it happened during that situation in 11th grade I mentioned earlier," she said.

"Who did the equal opposite in that exact moment?" I asked. "Who supported you financially and emotionally?"

"Me," mumbled Anna, without much thought, her eyes cast downward.

"In this context, that is not the answer we're looking for, Anna."

"Why not?" she asked, lifting her gaze from the floor and looking at me with a puzzled expression.

"If the force bringing you the challenge comes from outside you, then to compensate for that challenge, you will find support from the outside that balances your perception. The law of synchronicity tells us that the inner compensates the inner, and the outer compensates the outer. In other words, if you give yourself a challenge, you also give yourself support. But if someone outside you gives you a challenge, someone else from the outside offers support."

"So, it wouldn't be correct to think that my father gave me a challenge and I gave myself support?"

"That response is not in line with our working philosophy because it would imply that, for you to be 'good,' someone else must be 'bad.' If we were to think this way, it would mean that someone would always play the role of the villain in your life. And we don't want that. If we affirmed this mindset, you would remain stuck in the victim narrative. You'd continue to say, 'I'm suffering because of someone else, but that makes me strong.' As a result, you wouldn't transcend duality and would remain trapped in the same story."

She became thoughtful once more, her eyes dropping to the floor. "Okay, I understand now."

"In that exact moment in your room, when you were in 11th grade and you perceived that your father didn't support you financially and emotionally, who did the equal opposite? Who supported you financially?"

"There was no one there—I was alone." She stiffened, her jaw set as she crossed her arms.

"Anna, even if there wasn't a physical presence, connect with the moment and see who offered you financial and emotional support in your development."

"What do you mean?"

"Tell me, where are you at that moment?"

"In my room."

"Where exactly? What do you see around you?"

"I'm on my bed—it's light outside."

"What are you wearing?"

"Orange pants and a grey, striped shirt." Her voice softened and her speech was visibly slower.

"What is the bed like? What's on it?"

"A soft blanket, like a quilt," she said, sounding almost wistful.

"What do you hear? What sounds are around you?"

"The window is open—I hear voices, cars, and birds chirping."

"Excellent. You're fully anchored in that moment. Now, please, pause in the frame where you perceive your father isn't supporting you financially and emotionally. Pause in that moment where you feel he's not supporting you. Have you found the moment?"

"Yes, I've paused it."

"Good. What would be the opposite of what your father is doing at that moment? What would he ideally do instead of not supporting you?"

"He would trust me and give me money to go to college."

"Stay in that moment, Anna. You're on the bed, in your orange pants and striped shirt, feeling the soft blanket and hearing the sounds around you. Stay there. Now, at this moment, who offers you financial support to go to college?"

"No one. There's no one there."

"Pause there. In this exact moment, when you perceive that your father isn't supporting you, who is doing the opposite? Who is offering you trust and financial support?"

The silence in the room was thick, and as I watched Anna's clenched fists, I realized that the emotions she had been holding inside were about to come to the surface. She unclenched her fists, her palms sweaty, her breath shallow.

Then she said, "My grandfather! His words were in my head telling me he would sell his land if that was needed and give me the money to go to college." She burst into tears. I felt a cold shiver down my spine. What a powerful and certain response!

This realization was very important for Anna. The moment she saw the support—especially from a man—she was freed from the polarization that made her believe only women supported her and men did not.

We continued with a series of synchronicities, but no more than 9. When we look for those moments of judgment to balance them with the law of synchronicity, we realize there are relatively few.

This simple realization is truly liberating because we understand that we've been telling ourselves lies our whole lives by generalizing and distorting reality. Until now, Anna had lived with the perception that men had never supported her, so these moments of realigning reality brought a profound and different understanding of life.

I wasn't very surprised when, at the end of the session, Anna told me, "Monica, I had support all along—how incredible! I can't believe how blind I've been to it. I was so attached to the idea that the support had to come from my father, that I ignored all other forms of support. My grandmother, my grandfather, my teachers—they were there for me this whole time."

"That's right, Anna. Nothing is missing. You have everything you need. It's just that sometimes the form in which you receive support isn't the one you expect."

"Yes—my father didn't support me the way I wanted, but that doesn't mean I wasn't supported. It's like I got stuck on a single idea and refused to see the rest."

"That's the main lesson. Sometimes we get so attached to a certain form or expectation that we lose sight of what we already have."

"Nothing is missing," she whispered, in wonder. "You're right, Monica. I had everything I needed, exactly in the form I needed it."

"And how does this discovery make you feel?" I asked her.

"Free. Light. And grateful." She closed her eyes for a brief moment, as if savoring the weightlessness of her inner state.

Two days later, Anna called me to say she had slept through the night for the first time in years. She also told me that she had received a call from her father that morning. For no reason at all, he called her to say that he wanted to see her. He'd never done that before.

"Monica," she said, "can you believe that he's never initiated a visit? Today was the first time he's ever done that!" It's amazing how when we change something within ourselves, those around us respond differently, often with newfound warmth and openness.

Anna's story reveals a powerful truth about the law of synchronicity: support is always present, but may be not in the form we expect. Her shift from resentment to gratitude, when she finally understood that she lacked nothing, serves as a reminder that seeing both support and challenge simultaneously transforms our perspective, offering a deeper sense of self-mastery.

The Great Discovery

Jung and Pauli's work was advanced further by my mentor, Dr. John Demartini, who developed the law of synchronicity as described in this chapter. His students often refer to it as "the great discovery" because it represents one of the most profound insights into human behavior.

Around 20 years ago, while working on his book *The Mystery of the Living Cell*, Dr. Demartini studied redox reactions—chemical processes involving the transfer of electrons between 2 entities. In these reactions, oxidation is the loss of electrons, while reduction is the gain of electrons.

He observed that oxidation and reduction are inseparable; one cannot occur without the other. This intrinsic balance in nature, seen in the redox reactions, inspired his realization that life reflects this constant interplay of dual forces. Every moment is a balance of opposites—support and challenge, pain and pleasure, benefits and drawbacks—perfectly in sync.

The implications are incredible. Just think—what would happen if people truly understood that every moment, no matter what they do, carries an equal balance of support and challenge, pain and pleasure?

What would happen to politics? Could leaders and citizens shift from a polarized mindset of "good versus bad" to a more balanced approach, recognizing that every policy carries benefits and drawbacks?

What would therapy look like? Would it be possible that instead of focusing solely on eliminating pain, therapists might assist clients to embrace the balance in their experiences, seeing how every struggle comes with hidden gifts? Maybe therapy would evolve into a practice of supporting individuals in uncovering the equal and opposite benefits of their perceived difficulties, which would create a profound sense of gratitude and resilience.

How would it transform education? Teachers might encourage students to think critically about dualities, showing them how things like success and failure, or ease and struggle, are connected. This could lead to a generation that is less afraid of mistakes and more open to exploring, innovating, and learning from both triumphs and setbacks.

What about relationships? People might approach connections with less judgment and more understanding, seeing that conflicts and harmony are 2 sides of the same coin. This perspective could reduce blame and increase empathy, leading to healthier, more balanced interactions.

In every domain, this realization that support and challenge exist in equal measure could lead to a profound shift in how we think, act, and connect with the world around us.

Practical Application

Now, since we reached the end of the chapter, it is time for a little practice.

1. Seeing the Other Side

First, think of a moment when you perceived someone criticized you. Get really present with that moment. What is around you—what colors, smells, sounds? What is the topic they criticized you about?

Next, define the opposite in that moment. What would've been the opposite towards you on the same topic?

Finally, identify who is doing the opposite, at the exact synchronous moment, on the exact same topic. It can be someone physically present or someone in your mind.

If you become fully present in the moment, the answer comes instantly. If it takes longer, something else is at play—such as not being truly present. Take a few deep breaths, deeply reconnect with the moment, and try again.

2. Learn More about the School of Universal Laws

Our most advanced program, the School of Universal Laws, trains students to apply the most powerful tools for dissolving emotional charges in a professional setting. With 6 months of daily practice and a strong emphasis on real-world application, this program is 80% practice and 20% theory.

You will learn how to identify the root cause of a problem, create a process to dissolve it, and guide the client from where they are to where they want to be—whether it's achieving a goal or solving a problem—in order to create lasting change.

If the stories in this book resonate with you and you feel inspired to guide others through transformation, visit our website to learn more about the School of Universal Laws and the path to becoming an FTP specialist.

InspiredLifeCircle.com/school-of-universal-laws

CHAPTER 7

THE LAW OF ERISTIC ESCALATION

Imposition of order equals escalation of chaos.
— Principia Discordia

Balancing the Goal

Seven years ago, I worked with an entrepreneur named Nick, a driven and focused individual with a sharp mind for business. He was determined to grow his IT company's revenue from $2.5 million to $6 million that year.

Nick had tried to grow his company the previous year and the year before that, but hadn't succeeded. The market was booming, clients were everywhere, and other IT companies were visibly expanding. His company, however, had remained nearly stagnant for 2 years. He began to doubt his entrepreneurial abilities and believed something was wrong with him. He reached out to me, suspecting that his mind held hidden reasons for not achieving his goal.

When someone desires something intensely, the most effective approach is to "balance" the goal. We do this to avoid falling under the law of eristic escalation and creating the opposite. On a practical level, it means balancing the individual's perception of the goal and supporting them in seeing both the benefits and drawbacks in equal measure, both quantitatively and qualitatively.

So I asked Nick, "What are the downsides of achieving your goal?" and "What are the benefits of staying at $2.5 million in revenue?" I kept alternating between these 2 questions.

There are 2 reasons why I ask these questions in such situations. First, to balance the goal. If it's not truly a goal for them, then the client will be able to let go of it mentally. If someone balances a goal and no longer desires it, it means it wasn't truly theirs. It was something borrowed from others and not genuinely aligned with their life.

Often, we see something appealing in friends' lives and want it for ourselves, but it's not truly aligned with us. For example, you see a friend with 6-pack abs and decide to set the same goal. But you're not willing to spend time every day working out or follow their strict diet. In such cases, I use the expression "injecting" others' priorities into our lives, which isn't sustainable and leads to frustration.

The second reason for these questions is that the balancing process helps uncover hidden reasons why someone isn't achieving their goal—whether there are beliefs or other factors preventing them from reaching it.

When I did this exercise with Nick, he admitted that he wanted to maintain a family-like atmosphere in his company. At one point, he said, "Rather than risk losing this close-knit environment, I'd prefer to stay where I am." I asked, "Nick, did you hear what you just said?" And he replied, "Yes, that's true."

During our sessions Nick discovered that growing the company in the past had been very painful for him. He faced 2 paradoxical and equally painful situations. Either he had employees without enough work between projects, or he had projects but not enough employees to deliver them.

These 2 scenarios are paradoxical. However, in his mind, he had registered pain when he had employees without work because he still had to pay them. On the other hand, when he had projects but not enough staff to deliver them, he and his team faced burnout. We balanced these 2 painful situations with 2 other laws: the law of duality and the law of synchronicity.

In the end, Nick achieved his goal by the year's end. He reached $6 million in revenue while maintaining the family culture within his company. This achievement was not only a financial milestone but also a great personal example for him about aligning his mind with his goals.

Definition of the Law of Eristic Escalation

The law of eristic escalation states that:

imposition of order equals escalation of chaos.[56]

This concept has its origins in chaos theory and mathematics, and its name derives from Eris, the Greek goddess of discord, strife, and chaos. While the principle is not always explicitly called the "law of eristic escalation," it has been explored by researchers attempting to understand the nature of chaotic systems.

In simpler terms, this law suggests that attempts to impose strict control or order on a chaotic system can paradoxically lead to even greater disorder. It highlights the idea that rigid efforts to eliminate chaos often exacerbate the very chaos they aim to suppress.

Here are 3 examples of how this law manifests:

1. Politics and Governance

A government implementing overly strict laws to control civil unrest might provoke greater resistance or rebellion.

2. Parenting

Parents who impose excessive rules on rebellious teenagers may inadvertently encourage more defiant behavior.

---

56 This phrase originates from *Principia Discordia*, a satirical and philosophical text that serves as the foundational document of Discordianism, a parody religion or philosophical movement centered around chaos, humor, and irreverence. It was first published in 1965 by Gregory Hill (under the pseudonym Malaclypse the Younger) and Kerry Wendell Thornley (as Omar Khayyam Ravenhurst).

3. Technology and Security

Attempts to enforce highly restrictive digital rights management on software or media often lead to increased hacking and piracy.

You might observe this principle in your daily life. For instance, imagine you decide you want your home to be spotless, and just as you finish tidying everything, your child spills a bowl of milk and cereal on the carpet. Or perhaps you drop a glass, and it shatters, leaving you with an unexpected mess to clean. These small occurrences illustrate how efforts to impose perfect order invite chaos.

This law also helps explain why revolutions are predictable. The strict order, discipline, and poverty imposed by a communist regime, for example, often lead to an equal and opposite reaction—a revolution. The oppression of one force inevitably strengthens its counterforce.

I often say, "There's no such thing as a rebellious child, just overly strict parents." Rebellious children are often the product of excessively strict parenting. In my experience, I haven't seen rebellious kids when parents had relaxed rules. This was the case with my daughter. Throughout her adolescence, I didn't face rebellion-related issues, likely because I avoided imposing overly strict rules. As a result, she had little reason to rebel.

So, the more we amplify one side, the more its opposite intensifies too—echoing Newton's third law, published in 1687:

> *every action has an equal and opposite reaction.*

Whenever a force acts in one direction, there is inevitably a complementary force acting in the opposite direction on the same object at the same time. This principle under-pins both the physical world and the dynamics of human behavior, demonstrating the universal balance between order and chaos.

Doing the Inner Work—or Not

Three years ago, an entrepreneur came to me struggling with overwhelming anxiety. Let's call him Sam. He had several significant projects on the horizon, each one involving high stakes, grand venues, large audiences, and premium pricing. The pressure was weighing heavily on him, and he knew he needed to address his anxiety to better cope with these challenges. His anxiety was rooted in his perception of future potential failures and painful outcomes. Anxiety, as we know, often stems from an anticipation of pain and fear of failure.

To address the issue, I began by probing his perspective and I asked 2 key questions: "What disadvantages would you face if the project succeeded?" and "What benefits would you gain if the project failed?"

The process was anything but smooth. Sam struggled to articulate answers. Even when he managed to respond, the answers felt intellectual rather than heartfelt—they were superficial answers.

Despite the challenges, I encouraged him to persist. In such explorations, the transformative power lies in the client making his own connections and insights. As a guide, I could support and nudge, but the breakthroughs needed to come from him.

At some point Sam recognized that his anxiety was tied to past failures that had caused him deep emotional pain. These unprocessed experiences left him paralyzed at the thought of repeating similar mistakes. But when I suggested we delve into and balance these past pains, he refused, concerned that the emotional toll would be too much to bear. After that session, he avoided further meetings with me for some time.

Despite the avoidance, Sam didn't entirely abandon the process. Being an extremely intelligent individual, he began working through the questions on his own. He continued to think of the drawbacks of achieving his goal and the potential benefits of not achieving it.

He later shared with me that although his self-directed effort provided some clarity, the unresolved fears rooted in his past continued to hinder his progress. Ultimately, when the time came to execute his projects, he fell short of achieving the high standards he had set for himself.

Even though he didn't meet his ambitious goals, there was a silver lining. His self-reflection and the balancing exercises he partially completed allowed him to process the outcome in a less judgmental way. Instead of harshly criticizing himself for not achieving the projects' full potential, he viewed the experience with more balance than before.

In essence, while he did not succeed in reaching his external objective and still felt considerable anxiety, he also made some progress in his internal journey. I'm certain that if he had chosen to go all the way and balanced his perceptions about past failures, he would have been in a very different place—and more prepared for future projects. When we do our inner work, we become increasingly able to approach challenges with a steadier heart and mind.

When You Want Something Badly, You Create Resistance

There was a time when I tried to convince a friend to join me for a family holiday. I was overly persistent, and she said something that struck me: "The more you persist, the more I resist." At the time, I didn't know about the law of eristic escalation, but her words stayed with me. They made me stop pushing, and eventually she decided to come by her own choice.

The principle is simple: the more you try to impose your will on someone, the more resistance you provoke in them. The greater your determination to make something happen, the more likely you are to generate opposition. This dynamic often plays out in our lives, sometimes without us realizing it.

Think of a time when you desperately wanted something, but it just wouldn't happen. You tried and tried, only to meet resistance at every turn. Then, eventually, you gave up. You truly detached from the outcome, thinking, "That's enough; it's not for me," and stopped desiring it altogether. Surprisingly, that's often the moment when what you wanted effortlessly materialized.

One common example is in relationships. When someone is desperate to find a partner, their strong desire can inadvertently repel potential matches. Even if they have a chance, their intense energy can ruin it. It's often when they finally accept being single and stop actively seeking a partner that the right person appears—when there's nothing left to lose.

Another example is with certain couples who try to conceive for many years. The more a woman focuses on wanting to get pregnant, the more stress and resistance she creates, sometimes making it less likely to happen. Yet, as soon as the couple gives up trying—perhaps even adopting a child or deciding to live without children—suddenly, they find themselves expecting. I've seen this pattern play out many times.

A similar dynamic can occur when someone is looking for a job. The more desperately they search, sending out applications and stressing over every interview, the more resistance they seem to encounter. Rejections pile up, and frustration grows. But often, as soon as they step back, take a break, and decide to focus on something else—be it a hobby, volunteering, or personal development—an opportunity arises unexpectedly. It's as though the act of letting go creates the space for the right job to find them.

This phenomenon illustrates the law of eristic escalation: the harder you push for something, the more resistance you generate, keeping what you want at a distance. The more force you apply, the more power you inadvertently give to the opposing force, escalating the pair of opposing forces.

The same principle applies to internal struggles. For example, when you tell yourself, "I'm going to stay calm today," or "I'll quit smoking right now," you often experience the opposite effect. You crave cigarettes more, or you start feeling more agitated. The same thing happens when one decides to stop eating sugar, only to find themselves obsessing over sweets. This internal resistance is just as potent as external resistance.

Wanting something isn't enough, and neither is superficially accepting the situation you find yourself in. True resolution comes when you reach a state of balance, where achieving or not achieving your goal feels the same. Whether your child cleans their room or doesn't, it no longer matters—not because you're forcing yourself to feel that way, but because you genuinely no longer see it as positive or negative. You've reached a point of neutrality.

In that moment of balance, creation begins. When you are centered, free from the resistance of attachment or aversion, things manifest with ease in your outer reality. This is the key to working harmoniously with the law of eristic escalation.

Neutralize the Positives, Not Only the Negatives

Some time ago, I worked on an extraordinary case with a client named Lucas, who approached me in January of that year. Lucas, a quick-witted, seasoned entrepreneur who was highly self-aware, was one of the few clients who had ever come to me with this unusual challenge. He said, "Monica, last year went incredibly well and I'm worried a correction will follow."

He was referring to that unease caused by an inner sense of imbalance. This is where our intuition kicks in, whispering, "It can't be all positive without some negatives—there's a correction coming."

Lucas looked concerned and said, "I don't know what to do." I smiled, reassuring him, "That's okay! Let's talk, because I know exactly what we need to do." I then asked him "What do you perceive you gained last year?" and he told me a few things.

Then I asked, "At the same time, what have you lost in equal measure? What was the opposite that you manifested in your business?" And we worked through various moments of perception, one by one.

For instance, he had successfully secured a major project he was proud of. So I asked, "Where did you experience loss in equal measure?" He briefly thought about it and said, "I lost the connection I had with certain people and the team's focus on research and development."

His company was among the top firms in the technology research and development field, and one of their main clients was NASA. Research and development was in their DNA. When he saw that they had drifted away from who they truly were so that they could deliver this big project, this disadvantage weighed heavily. It hurt him when he realized they had distanced themselves from the research side, which he loved.

Then he continued with other drawbacks, finding them with little effort: "I lost opportunities on smaller projects that provided stability for the company. When we won this big project, almost all our resources went there. This project now accounts for more than 40 percent of our revenue, which is not healthy—having such a large percentage from a single client. So, I lost the stability the company had before."

We took each of the perceived achievements and balanced them. The goal wasn't to leave him mentally exhausted and saying, "Wow, I've had a horrible year." The goal was for him to see the balance so he wouldn't create a correction in the future. We found drawbacks until he could see that the benefits and drawbacks were equal.

The result was that he started the year with objectivity. The foundation from which he set his goals was balanced and grounded. It wasn't a manic state of "Wow, what a great year we had—let's aim for even more," as people tend to do, and often attract the opposite experience.

That year, he shifted his focus to research and development, allocating resources to support it and pursuing solutions aligned with their core strengths. This approach kept him at the forefront of IT research firms, and they had an even better year than before—thanks to the balancing process that helped him reconnect with what truly mattered to him.

The True Purpose of the Law of Eristic Escalation

In moments when you are poised and centered, when you achieve perfect balance, you don't experience desire. In those moments, you are deeply connected with your soul. These are the moments when you have perfect clarity about the future. This isn't about projecting into the future—it's about knowing it. Simultaneously, your past becomes clear, unburdened by regret or judgment. You recognize how everything that happened was aligned to lead you to this moment.

When you are centered, you are not in a state of wanting—instead, you simply know. There is certainty in this state. However, the moment you desire something, you get back into the default mode—whether seeking a positive outcome or avoiding a negative one. The act of wanting inherently involves a duality—wanting something positive means there is a negative counterpart you wish to avoid, and vice versa. These 2 sides are intrinsically connected. When you oscillate between seeking the positive and avoiding the negative, you don't have balance and you are no longer centered. This unbalanced state leads to reactive behavior.

To get you back to a place of balance, you will find yourself encountering the opposite of what you desire. This is the true purpose of the law of eristic escalation. It serves as an internal and external mechanism to bring you back to your center, guiding you toward balance. There is no mistake in this process; it is an invitation to realign with yourself.

The more you desire to obtain that positive thing, the more you attract the negative one. The fact that you keep dating the same type of individuals, attracting the same type of employer, the same type of client, or the same type of employee you wish to avoid—and this causes you pain—is simply a profound invitation to center your perception and return to balance.

You might think, "If I stop wanting money, will I attract it?" If you are genuinely aligned with the idea of not desiring money and you are truly centered, then abundance can naturally flow to you. It's not about rejecting money but about reaching a state of centeredness. From this place, you will experience gratitude for what is. This balanced state is the foundation from which you can build your future.

The ultimate goal of the law of eristic escalation is to bring you back to balance and centeredness so you can become the master of your destiny. When you are centered and aligned, you transcend the state of wanting. In the state of perfect alignment with your soul, your mission, and with

God, there is no desire, no "seeking and avoiding." Instead, there is a deep knowing and certainty.

Desire exists only in a polarized state, where you are caught between avoiding the negative and seeking the positive. In a balanced state, spontaneous action emerges from inspiration, not from desire. Sophia's story below offers a clear example of how this principle plays out.

Much of today's world operates from a place of "I want." But the subtle difference between acting from inspiration and acting from desire is profound. It is this nuance that defines the transition from a reactive, unbalanced state to a centered, inspired existence.

Why Balancing Your Goals Matters

Last spring, another FTP specialist, my colleague Michael, worked with a client named Sophia, one of the most skilled business consultants I've ever met. She had ambitious goals for the year. She wanted to grow her business, build an extraordinary reputation, and attract high-level clients.

At their first session, Sophia leaned forward, her eyes wide with determination. "I've set big goals this year. I'm ready to make them happen, " she said with conviction in her voice. Michael nodded. "That's fantastic. Before we dive into strategies on how to achieve that, let's balance your goals."

Sophia frowned, visibly annoyed. "Balance? What do you mean by that? These goals are my priorities. They're non-negotiable."

"It means we'll explore the other side of your goals—what they might cost you and what you're giving up by pursuing them. It's about seeing the full picture," Michael explained.

Sophia crossed her arms, her face set in a firm expression. "I don't see why that's necessary. I know what I want. There's nothing wrong with my goals." Sophia's body language spoke volumes—she resisted balancing her goals worse than a lovesick teenager, unwilling to see any flaw in her new obsession. But as Michael gently pressed, his calm confidence made it harder to dismiss the questions outright. His words lingered, planting seeds of awareness that took root.

"You might not see all the downsides yet, but I promise this process will help you gain clarity," Michael said. "Let's start with this: What are the drawbacks of achieving your first goal?" Sophia hesitated, still unwilling to see disadvantages. "Drawbacks? None. These goals are great."

But then a flicker of realization appeared on her face. She uncrossed her arms. Maybe there was something she hadn't considered. Her answers became less defensive, more reflective. "I suppose—if I grow too fast, I might lose personal connection with my clients," she admitted.

"That's a good start," Michael encouraged. "Now, what benefits would you gain if you stayed at this level?" Sophia sighed. "I will have more time for myself. I used to love gardening, but now I'm so busy I never touch my plants."

They worked through the process layer by layer. "What's the drawback of being recognized by the type of entrepreneurs you're targeting?" Michael continued to ask. Sophia thought for a moment. "They're high achievers, but—they are difficult to work with. Some of them might just see me as a tool, not a partner."

"And what about the financial goals you've set? Any downsides to achieving them?" Michael asked. Sophia paused. "If I'm being honest, I might lose sight of what's meaningful to me. I don't want to become someone who's all about image and no substance."

"And what are the downsides of working with extremely ambitious, high-achieving entrepreneurs?" asked Michael. Through these questions, Sophia realized something profound. "I don't actually want a huge business at any cost," she said. "What I want is to do something meaningful, something that aligns with my philosophy of balance."

Michael was listening carefully. "That's a powerful insight. What does that balance look like for you?" Sophia's eyes grew wider as the words left her lips, as if hearing them aloud strengthened something deep within her. She paused, the realization settling in like a missing puzzle piece clicking into place. "It's about helping clients who want authenticity," Sophia replied. "I want to support people who are working on things that truly inspire them, not just doing what they 'have to.'"

As Sophia gained this clarity, her perspective shifted. She began evaluating achievement and failure differently. "I see now that the direction I was striving for wasn't sustainable for me," she admitted.

In the months that followed, everything started to align. "The quality of my clients is so much better now," Sophia shared during a follow-up session. "I'm attracting people who truly value what I offer." She also made difficult choices, parting ways with clients who displayed an attitude of "I'm hiring you to do the work for me, but I'm not willing to put in any effort myself."

Six months after she started working with Michael, she founded a new business focused on social entrepreneurship, which was perfectly aligned with her philosophy on life. In this new business, Sophia supports other small business owners who generate growth and sustainability locally by encouraging production within communities.

For instance, a business sourcing coffee beans from a rural village might pay fair wages, provide training, and reinvest in community projects like schools or healthcare. Beyond economics, Sophia's approach strengthens social cohesion by creating a shared sense of purpose that uplifts the entire ecosystem.

The Law of Eristic Escalation in the Realm of Healing

Having dealt with frequent migraines, I've come to realize that the real issue isn't the pain itself—it's the resistance to it. When we focus on our physical body during pain or illness, there's a natural instinct to fight it. We tense up, and that internal struggle only intensifies the discomfort.

One of the biggest breakthroughs in my healing process was understanding that healing isn't something you do—it's something you receive. Healing requires stepping out of the control mindset and stepping into a state of receptivity.

A key realization here is that you can't return to a previous version of health. The expectation to restore your body to the exact condition it once was is unrealistic because you're constantly evolving. The new version of yourself incorporates all your experiences, including illness. Often, the illness itself carries the solution. It's not an enemy to be eradicated but a message to be received.

When you shift your perspective and see illness—be it a migraine or something else—as a solution rather than a problem, the fight dissolves. Instead of resisting the pain, you receive it, stay with it, and listen to what it's telling you. In this receptive state, the pain often disappears. The act of no longer fighting is what allows healing to occur.

This dynamic is the law of eristic escalation at work: the more you resist or fight against something, the more power you give it. Conversely, when you stop fighting, the tension dissipates, and balance is restored. Healing doesn't come from understanding why you have a migraine or merely accepting its presence. It happens when you go deeper— when you find that inner space of true balance and recognize the pain not as a problem, but as part of your journey. That's when gratitude for the experience surfaces, and real healing begins.

6 Principles of the Law of Eristic Escalation

These 6 principles outline how repressed material— whether emotional, behavioral, or cultural—inevitably resurfaces, often through conflict or crisis. But seen clearly, each escalation offers a path to integration and balance.

1. What You Repress Will Explode
Repression leads to eventual expression—often in destructive or chaotic ways. When emotional explosions occur in

someone's life, they can usually be traced back to unresolved issues or unacknowledged emotions that were suppressed over time. Identifying and addressing these areas of repression can help prevent these types of explosions and bring balance.

2. Whatever Parents Repress, Children Express

Children have an uncanny ability to mirror their parents' unresolved and suppressed issues. If you notice a behavior that you don't like in your child, consider looking inward to uncover what you might be repressing as a parent.

Instead of reacting, take it as an opportunity to see what needs attention within you. By working through your own repressed emotions or actions and allowing them to be expressed in a healthy way, your child will no longer need to express them on your behalf.

For instance, many parents told me they were concerned about their teenager's high interest in sex. At the same time this was one aspect of their own life that they were repressing. So if you don't want your children to have sex at a young age, make sure you don't repress sex. If you repress it, they will express it.

3. What General Society Represses, Selective Society Expresses

There will always be small groups or subcultures expressing the very things that mainstream society suppresses. These expressions act as a mirror, showcasing what the collective majority has avoided or rejected.

For example, countercultural movements often arise to challenge societal norms. Punk culture expressed rebellion against conformity, avant-garde art expressed ideas rejected by traditional aesthetics, and LGBTQ+ communities have often been at the forefront of expressing identities and orientations suppressed by conventional societal norms. These groups play a vital role in bringing balance and fostering dialogue about what society at large has repressed.

4. The More You Want Something, the More It Becomes Out of Reach

Desperation or excessive attachment to outcomes creates resistance. This principle highlights the paradox of desire—the more you want something, the further away the desired outcome seems. Letting go of attachment makes space for a more natural alignment with what you seek.

5. You Cannot Escape What You Fear

Fear has a magnetic quality. When you focus on running away from something you fear, you're likely to draw that very thing into your life. This principle suggests that balancing the perception of fear is the key to neutralizing its influence.

6. Unloved and Unbalanced Things Will Reappear

Everything you reject or judge without love will continue to show up in your life. These recurring patterns are an invitation to integrate and reconcile what has been rejected.

This principle ties into the law of fractals (see chapter 9)—the idea that the unloved aspects of life create patterns that repeat until they are brought into harmony. These patterns are interconnected and often reflect deeper, unacknowledged dynamics in your life. By seeing both sides and loving these aspects, you break the cycle and restore balance.

Practical Application

Ready to apply what you've learned? Here are 2 exercises to do that.

1. Balance a Goal

Choose a goal or a result you want to achieve. It can be personal or business.

- Write down at least 25 drawbacks of achieving your goal.
- Write down at least 25 benefits of not achieving your goal—of remaining in your current situation.

The reason I'm asking for more than 25 benefits and drawbacks is to push your mind to think beyond what you already know consciously. Most people will find the first 5 to 10 answers rapidly if they're not overly attached to it. But these will not make new connections in your mind. Staying with the discomfort of not knowing the answer and searching for it within your mind is where the magic happens.

When you identify the drawbacks of achieving a goal and the benefits of not achieving it, you make your mind more flexible, view the goal with greater objectivity and perspective, and increase your chances of bringing it to fruition. That's the first benefit. The second is that, by being more flexible about reaching your goal, you begin to see alternatives—new paths, actions, and opportunities—that weren't visible to you when you were attached to achieving it.

2. Become Aware of a Repressing and Expressing Dynamic

Think of something you've been repressing that your children may be expressing for you.

Maybe you're not very interested in fashion—so they constantly bring it to your attention. Perhaps your social life isn't a priority, and your teenager reflects that by going out often. Or maybe you've forgotten to play, become too serious, and now your son is obsessed with video games. What is it in your case?

If you don't have children, you can explore this dynamic with your life partner, business partner, or team members.

Once you've identified an example of repression and expression in your life, look for a time in the past when you were least repressing that aspect. Was your child or partner expressing it less during that same period?

After identifying the dynamic between repression and expression, you can apply the law of reflection by owning the traits you don't want others to express so strongly. For instance, if you don't want your kids to go out to parties so often, schedule your own outings—go out partying with your husband or friends.

CHAPTER 8

THE LAW OF ORDER

We no longer use the term "disorder" but instead we distinguish between different degrees of order.

— David Bohm[57]

Rainmakers, Diamonds, and Miracles

There is an old story about a region where people were suffering from severe drought. For 3 long years, there was no rain. The people cried, prayed, and waited, but nothing happened. Then, they heard about a wise man—a rainmaker—who was said to have the ability to bring rain wherever he went. Desperate, they sought him out and brought him to their community.

The rainmaker arrived and set up his tent in the middle of the village. He stayed inside for 3 days, doing nothing that

---

57 David Bohm, *Wholeness and the Implicate Order* (Routledge, 1980), 149.

was visible to the villagers. On the third day, it rained. The people were overjoyed. They celebrated the long-awaited rain and then approached the rainmaker to ask, "What did you do?"

He replied, "I brought order to my inner world, and then the outer world responded with its own order—and something normal happened. It rained."

We've all experienced times when we felt stuck, like the villagers suffering through their drought. We tried everything we could, but nothing seemed to work. Then, seemingly out of nowhere, someone asked us a great question—a question that opened the heavens. Suddenly clarity came, and progress resumed—like rain after a long dry spell.

When you ask the right questions, you become a rainmaker for yourself and for others. You become a modern-day Socrates, assisting those around you to uncover the greatest answers within themselves.

When my husband Stefan was a teenager, he had his own Socrates—a physics teacher who became his mentor. He was teaching in another high school, and he certainly didn't fit the mold of a conventional teacher. One day, he explained to young Stefan what happens at the atomic level when a "miracle" occurs. Specifically, he described what happens to atoms and molecules when someone experiences what we call a "miraculous" healing.

"Do you know what a diamond is made of?" the teacher asked during one of their walks.

"No, I don't," Stefan replied.

"How about graphite?"

"Carbon?" the young man asked shyly.

"They are both pure carbon," the teacher smiled, then explained, "The only difference is their atomic structure. In a diamond, the structure has more order. In graphite, there is less order. One is the hardest substance on earth, and the other can be shattered with your fingers. Think about it—the only difference is how the information is organized. Nothing else."

He then explained how some people had experienced miraculous healings in the past. Across different cultures, there were wise men and women believed to possess the power to perform miracles. But, according to the old physics teacher, they didn't possess any supernatural powers.

Rather, they had a higher degree of internal order because the information within themselves was organized differently. When an individual with less order came into their presence, their internal structure—even at the molecular and atomic levels—aligned to the higher order, much like the parable of the rainmaker.

Isn't it interesting that we refer to many forms of illness as a *disorder*? The dictionary defines *disorder* as both "a state of confusion, a mess, chaos" and "an illness that disrupts normal physical or mental functions."

When you learn to apply the universal laws of math and physics to human behavior, you support others to reorganize the information within and become stronger. Sometimes, this reorganization leads to healing. Other times, it sparks business innovations or creates harmony in relationships.

You can apply this to your own mind, too. Asking yourself the right questions builds a stronger and brighter mind, much like the structure of a diamond. Conversely, asking the wrong questions makes your mind fragile, like graphite. That's why it can be said that the quality of your life depends on the quality of the questions you ask yourself.

Definition of the Law of Order

The law of order says that

higher order attracts and organizes lower levels of order.

Consider the following example. If you are a competent finance manager, so obsessed with work that you neglect health and fitness, you will look up to a fitness instructor and take in their advice. If they are competent, they may easily become the authority or the leader for you in terms of health and fitness because they have a higher level of order in that area of life. On the other hand, the fitness instructor has lower order when it comes to money, and they will look up to you when it comes to personal finances. You are the leader for them in this area, because you have a higher degree of order when it comes to managing money. So, at a personal level, order is contextual, as you will see in this chapter. But how about larger systems?

Anyone who's ever owned a large house or a spacious garden knows that it takes significantly more effort to maintain everything and prevent it from deteriorating. If your garden is just a few square meters, you don't need much planning or many tools to create a beautiful, thriving corner. But if your garden spans a few acres, maintaining it requires coordinated effort, thoughtful planning, and the right tools throughout the year. In the same way, every system with greater mass operates with a higher internal order—one that might not be immediately visible, but is always present beyond what meets the eye.

Order in the Solar System

From a thermodynamic perspective, *order* can be understood as a state of lower entropy. Systems with higher mass, like the sun or the earth, have more structured and sustained processes, which might be interpreted as "lower entropy" or "higher order."

The sun sustains nuclear fusion, producing immense energy and maintaining a highly organized structure over billions of years. In contrast, planets are recipients of the sun's energy and lack such dynamic internal processes. The sun's gravitational field also imposes a structured order on the planets, confining their orbits into predictable paths.

Similarly, the earth supports life, has a hydrosphere and atmosphere, and is geologically active. These features make earth more "ordered" compared to the moon, which lacks atmosphere, liquid water, and geological activity.[58] Earth's gravitational influence organizes the moon into a stable orbit, reducing potential chaos in its trajectory.

In a metaphorical sense, the "higher order" of systems like the sun or the earth attracts "lower-order" systems like planets or the moon. The gravitational and energetic dominance of the larger system imposes structure and stability on the smaller, less ordered system. This mirrors how orga-

---

58 The moon is not geologically active in the way the earth is—there are no active volcanoes or large-scale tectonic plate movements. It does exhibit some minor geological activity, however, which is often referred to as being "seismically active."

nized systems often stabilize and integrate less organized ones in physical, social, or biological contexts.

Order in Geopolitical Dynamics

Throughout history, empires have risen by bringing order and structure to the world. The Roman Empire, for example, is renowned for building roads, bridges, aqueducts, and even a postal service—systems that shaped the foundation of modern infrastructure. At the time, being a Roman citizen was a significant privilege, much like being an American or UAE citizen today. One could argue that the Roman Empire developed such organized systems precisely because it was a vast and complex structure. Or, perhaps we recognize it as a large and powerful system because of its high degree of order and organization.

Historically, empires have had colonies across the globe, gravitating around the imperial center like planets around the sun. These colonies learned and grew in order and organization, drawing from the empire's knowledge. When a colony developed its own internal systems and reached a higher level of order than the empire itself, the balance shifted—and independence became inevitable. This was the case with the United States, whose Declaration of Independence in 1776 officially signaled to the world that it no longer needed the structure of the British Empire to govern itself.

Countries with more order and organization attract and influence those with less. Developing nations often look up to highly organized countries like Germany, renowned for its efficiency, governance, and systems. Germany's approaches to infrastructure, renewable energy, and vocational education have been widely studied and emulated.

For instance, nations with less-developed apprenticeship systems have modeled their frameworks after Germany's highly-structured dual education system.[59] By adopting these principles, they aim to enhance workforce skills and economic stability. This illustrates how countries with lower levels of order often adopt systems and principles from more organized nations to improve their own structures.

Order in the Business World

Large companies like Google naturally attract—and often acquire—smaller companies such as YouTube, Android, or Waze. Once integrated, these smaller entities function like planets within Google's larger "solar system": they orbit around a central force while still maintaining their own unique ecosystems and operational rhythms.

A company with a higher level of internal order will influence companies with lower levels of order. Consider how businesses worldwide study the history of Apple, striving to incorporate its principles and culture. Apple's structured approach to design, technology, and user experience has set a benchmark. Conversely, Nokia's failure to adapt when the iPhone launched is an example of how a lack of internal order or alignment can lead to downfall. Nokia's inability to reorganize its priorities and innovate in response to Apple's structured approach serves as a cautionary tale.

---

59 Germany's dual education system combines classroom-based learning with practical, on-the-job training. It allows students—typically starting around age 16—to split their time between vocational schools (Berufsschule) and working at a company. This system usually lasts 2 to 3 years and is most common in technical and skilled trades like engineering, manufacturing, IT, and healthcare. Students gain both theoretical knowledge and hands-on experience, often earning a small salary during training. The dual system is widely regarded as a key factor in Germany's low youth unemployment and strong industrial workforce, as it aligns education closely with market needs.

When a company has alignment between their own products and processes and what their clients want, we can say that it has order. When there is misalignment, we notice chaos. We are attracted to order and repelled by chaos.

A startup usually begins with a leader—or a small group—who carry a clear vision of what they want to build. Other team members are drawn to that vision, naturally gravitating around them like planets orbiting the sun. And the success of that venture? It is directly proportional to the level of internal order the leader brings.

Individual Order and Alignment

On an individual level we are attracted to this internal sense of order and alignment. When someone has cultivated internal order in a specific domain, they naturally attract others who have less order in that area.

Consider a chef who is world-renowned for their impeccable culinary skills and well-organized kitchen. Their mastery of flavors, precise techniques, and systematic approach to preparing dishes naturally attract aspiring cooks or even seasoned chefs looking to refine their craft. If this same chef struggles with business skills, however, they might turn to someone with greater order in those areas—like a business coach or entrepreneur.

Order is not merely about visual symmetry or external arrangement. The order we are talking about here resides in the invisible realm—something we experience internally. Recognizing it allows us to understand how it shapes our external results and drives our overall evolution.

Think about a moment in the last 2 years when you worked with someone who was really on top of their game. Did you find it? Maybe it was a doctor who treated you, a colleague at work, or a handyman who came to fix something around the house. You could feel their level of order—the way they moved through their work with clarity and ease. Things that seemed complicated to you were solved quickly, without drama. That's what order looks like in everyday life. It feels smooth, efficient, even energizing.

If you want more energy in your life, surround yourself with people who operate like that: people with higher levels of order in their work. And be careful about working with those who operate in lower levels of order—because it will cost you more than you think.

When to Use the Law of Order

After people understand what the law of order is about, they often say to me, "Monica, this sounds great, but what do you use it for? In what situations do you apply this law?" That's a great question. The short answer is: the law of order is best applied when you want to achieve a new and challenging goal. Let me explain.

Imagine you're aiming for a bold new financial goal in your business—maybe doubling your revenue or launching a new high-ticket offer. That doesn't happen by simply working harder—you need to become the kind of person who naturally operates at that level. That might mean thinking more strategically, setting clearer boundaries, or leading with greater confidence. If you had already embodied that version of yourself, the results would already be showing.

It's that next-level identity—with a higher degree of internal order—that aligns your actions, decisions, and mindset to actually create the breakthrough.

In 1948, Claude Shannon, the father of information theory, gave humanity a critical insight: disorder is *missing information*.[60] He defined entropy (disorder) as a measure of uncertainty, or randomness—the opposite of certainty and expected outcomes. In our example above, it means you're missing information to become the next-level identity. That version of you sees the whole picture about the goal. That version of you doesn't guess or hope, but has clarity and certainty.

I have 2 annoying questions for entrepreneurs who come to me with big ambitious goals: (1) What are the benefits of you not achieving the goal? and (2) What drawbacks would you have if you were to achieve this goal? Most people hate these questions because they don't understand their power. They only see the positives of the goal and very few negatives, if any. They only see half of the picture. The *missing information* is precisely what holds them in the same cycle, preventing them from achieving the results they want. That's why most people are wandering around in circles for years, mistaking motion for progress.

I've worked with women who deeply wanted to have children but couldn't, despite being physically healthy and undergoing numerous treatments. In these cases, we use a

---

60 Claude E. Shannon, "A Mathematical Theory of Communication," *Bell System Technical Journal* 27, no. 3 (July 1948): 392–93. The exact quote is: "From our previous discussion of entropy as a measure of uncertainty it seems reasonable to use the conditional entropy of the message, knowing the received signal, as a measure of this missing information. This is indeed the proper definition, as we shall see later."

specific protocol designed to uncover the hidden dynamics that may be at play. Two of the most important questions we ask are (1) What are the benefits of not having a child? and (2) What would be the drawbacks if you were to have a baby? These questions are not probing for the obvious or superficial answers—but the real, personal, and often unconscious costs tied to the woman's unique life situation.

You'd be surprised how difficult it is for many women to answer these questions. Up to that point they only saw the dream—the beautiful, loving, easy experience of motherhood. But when someone sees only benefits and none of the challenges, they're caught in infatuation. And one of the silent plagues of modern society is postpartum depression. It affects at least 1 in 5 new mothers and, in severe cases, includes heavy suicidal thoughts.[61] From my perspective, this depression is often a direct consequence of that earlier infatuation. The higher a woman's expectations were—if she only saw joy, connection, and ease in motherhood—the more likely she is to crash emotionally when the real experience includes struggle, exhaustion, or identity shifts. Depression is a by-product of infatuation. You experience depression when your reality doesn't match your fantasy. In other words, your world is not "what it was supposed to be" in your mind.

The same pattern shows up with many first-time entrepreneurs. Imagine someone who excelled in a technical job and then they left to start their own business. They imagined total freedom—doing only what they love, earning more, living on their own terms. But soon they discover they're

---

61 Ziyi Wang et al., "Mapping global prevalence of depression among postpartum women," *Translational Psychiatry* 11 (2021): 543, https://doi.org/10.1038/s41398-021-01663-6.

working twice as much, earning far less, and juggling roles they never wanted: bookkeeping, sales, marketing, management, and so on. When reality doesn't match the fantasy, they feel disillusioned and depressed. Again, the missing piece was a realistic understanding of both sides.

Whether it's motherhood or business, missing information creates disorder—defined in the dictionary as "a state of confusion" or "a condition that disrupts normal physical or mental functions."

Order means to see both sides of a situation, positive and negative, in equal measure. As the law of duality states, the whole is made of complementary opposites. You can't have order if you don't see the whole picture. The more you see from the whole, in any context, the more order you have. And the more order you have, the closer you are to achieve the goals at that level. That's why we say:

You can only manifest up to the level of order you hold inside.

Order, Chaos, and the Courage to Choose Yourself

I had the privilege of working with a client, Carmen, who was developing a franchise network at the time. That's where our work together began.

Carmen started with one restaurant that was thriving. It wasn't successful by accident—she had a clear vision for it. She loved being there. She loved creating the atmosphere, connecting directly with the staff, chatting with the customers, and curating a space where people felt great. Her restaurant quickly became the number one place in town. On weekends, it was the go-to spot for families with kids.

During the week, it was the preferred meeting place for professionals.

Over time, friends began encouraging her: "What if you created a franchise? What if you scaled this success?" She thought about it. Reflected on it. Eventually, she said yes. And like any responsible businesswoman, she brought in consultants to support the expansion. She began opening new restaurants in different cities through a franchise model, and even considered going international, thinking about major cities across Europe.

But by the time Carmen came to me, something felt off and she was torn. She couldn't find her place anymore. On one hand, she felt the pressure of overseeing the original restaurant and the new locations. On the other hand, she was being pulled toward building out the franchise. She couldn't do both the way she wanted.

We started by clarifying her big vision—what she truly wanted to create. We examined how the organization needed to function at scale, just like her kitchen did in the early days. The ordering systems, the supplier logistics, the marketing and sales engine—this time, not for one location but for an entire network. That shift in perspective brought a huge realization: she already knew how to do this. Just like she had designed the kitchen and the service flow for her restaurant, she could design the back-end systems for the franchise.

Then I asked her the deeper question: "Who do you need to become to bring this vision to life?" Because she could no longer be the kind, warm owner welcoming guests and overseeing orders in person. That version of her couldn't scale. She needed to shift into a new identity.

Then came a turning point. Carmen realized the idea of building a franchise didn't actually inspire her. It would mean giving up that direct connection—the people, the energy, the soul of her restaurant. It would be a different business altogether. And she wasn't inspired about it.

So she made a conscious and courageous choice: instead of building a mediocre franchise, she would pour herself into maintaining the best restaurant in the city. She saw clearly what was aligned with her heart, and what brought her true fulfillment. She recognized that she simply didn't have the same energy for scaling a franchise as she did when she built her own place from the ground up.

Carmen was honest with herself. She knew that no matter how successful the franchise might become, she wouldn't feel the same deep satisfaction from that as she did from seeing her customers leave her restaurant satisfied and grateful.

And because she chose inner alignment and order, she kept her restaurant at the top—even as many new ones opened in the meantime.

Carmen's story is a powerful reminder: you can only manifest up to the level of order you hold inside. She had order for one restaurant, but not for a national or international franchise. And rather than forcing herself to become someone she wasn't—someone others told her she should be—she honored what was real within her.

Because all those outside opinions were just noise. Well-meaning, of course, but ultimately a distraction that would have resulted in chaos.

Internal Order, the Essence of Leadership

Dictionaries define *leadership* as the quality or ability that makes an individual a leader. But it's one of those words that, if you ask 3 people at a table, you'll get 5 different meanings. One individual might say it's charisma, another might insist it's innate, yet another would argue it's a skill that can be developed—and so on.

In my experience, leadership is contextual and is about the level of internal order one has in a particular area. The individual with the highest order in that area will lead. If your doctor has greater order in health and fitness, you'll follow their guidance in that domain. If your teenager has higher order when it comes to fashion, you will follow them when you buy shoes. If a 25-year-old has a higher order about technology and AI, you will follow their tech advice. And each of *them* might follow *you* in other areas where you have more order and organization than they have.

What do the doctor, the teenager, and the 25-year-old have in common? They see more of the whole picture in their area of expertise than other people do—both the positives and the negatives. Would you agree that a doctor knows not only the benefits of a medicine but also its contraindications and side effects? Only when they understand both can they prescribe it with confidence. A true master knows that every solution creates a problem and every problem has the solution in it, as the ancient Chinese have illustrated in the yin-yang symbol. Your ability to hold paradoxes in your mind is a measure of your leadership in a particular area of life.

From a leadership perspective, there are 3 important aspects of the law of order. First, order means seeing the whole, with both sides. Second, order requires you to own both sides. And third, order is about how many details you hold in your vision. We discussed the first aspect already, so let's talk about the second and third.

Order means to own both sides. In other words, your leadership is limited by your capacity to own your dark side. If you try to be only kind, honest, and hard-working yet reject your aggressiveness, dishonesty, or laziness, you are limiting your leadership. I know it may sound crazy and counterintuitive, but it's true. World leaders are ok to be hated by half the population, while other people can't sleep if their neighbor is upset with them.

Order is also about how many details you hold in your vision. The more vivid and detailed your vision—especially if those details are written down—the greater your chances are of manifesting it.[62] Now imagine you're organizing an event for 200 people. Any detail you overlook will cause problems later. Any loose ends can create chaos down the line. But if you envision everything—how guests are greeted, who welcomes them, how they find their seats, and how the event flows moment by moment—that internal order will translate into an extraordinary external experience.

Great artists and scientists throughout history—like Leonardo da Vinci, Thomas Edison, and Buckminster Fuller—had the ability to visualize an extraordinary level of detail in their minds before creating anything physical or even putting it on paper. For instance, Nikola Tesla said "I do not rush into actual work. When I get an idea, I start at once building it up in my imagination. [...] Without ever having

---

62 I recommend Cameron Herold's book, *Vivid Vision*, for those who are interested in building a vision for their company or for their personal life. It's a
great step-by-step framework with practical examples.

drawn a sketch I can give the measurements of all parts to workmen, and when completed all these parts will fit, just as certainly as though I had made the actual drawings."[63]

You might think this is a trait reserved for great geniuses that you don't possess—but that's simply not true. These people were able to see so many details in their minds because they spent a lot of time with the problem. Most people think about an issue for a few minutes, then give up and say they couldn't find the answer. But it's amazing what your mind can do if you spend just 2 focused hours with a problem. You'd be surprised how often a solution emerges—usually within that time—if you give it your full, undivided attention after a good night's sleep.

I learned this from my friend Raz, who shared his practice of "staying with the problem" inspired by a quote widely attributed to Albert Einstein: "It's not that I'm so smart, it's just that I stay with problems longer." My husband, Stefan, follows a similar personal rule: if he can't solve a problem on his own within 2 hours, he'll then seek support from others. But first, he stays with the problem—and most of the time, he finds the next step.

This is a practical technique to create more internal order and increase your leadership. Try it. You'll be surprised how few problems remain unsolved when you give them just 2 hours of focused attention.

---

63 Nikola Tesla, "My Early Life," *My Inventions: The Autobiography of Nikola Tesla*, ed. Ben Johnston (Experimenter Publishing Co., 1919).

Brain Science and the Law of Order

Another scientific discovery that supports the law of order is the reticular activating system (RAS), which was identified through a series of studies in the mid-20th century. It explains how the mind prioritizes information from most important to least important, and why people have varying degrees of order in different areas of their lives.

The RAS is a network of neurons located in the brainstem, specifically in the reticular formation, that plays a crucial role in regulating attention. It acts as a gatekeeper, filtering the vast amount of sensory information your brain receives and determining what is important enough to reach your conscious awareness. Simply put, it filters what you see and hear, prioritizing what is important and suppressing irrelevant data.

Here's a practical, relatable example to demonstrate how it works in everyday life. Let's say you've decided to buy a red Toyota. Before making the decision, you rarely noticed Toyotas on the road, and if you did, you didn't pay much attention to their color. But now that you're excited about buying one, it seems like every tenth car you see is a red Toyota. Suddenly, you're spotting them in parking lots, commercials, and they're even coming up in conversations.

Did the number of red Toyotas actually increase? Of course not! Your reticular activating system went to work prioritizing anything related to a red Toyota because it's now important to you. Your brain is filtering out irrelevant stimuli (e.g., other car types and colors) and making you more aware of what aligns with your focus or interest.

The RAS organizes information based on priority and significance. Once your brain perceives something as important
(like a goal, interest, or emotional connection), the RAS
tunes into anything related to it. This explains why people
have higher levels of order in the areas that are important
to them, which we will explore in the next section.

When you see things as being *on the way* rather than *in the
way*, when you notice synchronicities and you connect the
dots effortlessly—that's a clear sign of higher levels of order.
On the other hand, when you feel stuck, lacking ideas, or like
nothing is flowing—these are all symptoms of a lower level
of order. Your brain operates differently when it comes to
higher and lower order, and it does this naturally based on
a precise hierarchy of priorities, unique to each individual.
Let's go deeper into what this means.

Priorities, the Key to Internal Order

You may be wondering by now how you cultivate more
internal order. That's a great question, so let's try a simple,
2-part exercise that will take about 5 minutes. Don't skip
this exercise—if you're not in a place where you can do it,
put the book down and come back to it when you can.

Part 1

Take a moment to remember something you did in the last
2 months that truly inspired you—when time seemed to
disappear, and you were fully present with what you were
doing. Don't stop until you find a specific moment—something real you actually did and loved it.

Now, let yourself feel the energy that was moving through your body in that moment. What did it feel like? Notice any physical sensations in your muscles, heart rate, or breathing. Notice any feelings you experience. Were your shoulders tense or relaxed? Did the action come from within you—or did it feel like someone else had to push you? Did the activity energize you, or did it drain you?

Be present with that experience. As you notice how it feels in your body, stay with it and become aware of the shift that happens in you simply by reconnecting to that moment of inspiration.

Did you do it? Great. Now move your body a bit to transition to part 2. Shake your arms, stretch your neck, bend your knees, and let's go to the second part.

Part 2

This time bring to mind an activity you did in the last 2 months that you felt you *had* to do. You didn't love it. Maybe it was asked of you, or maybe you told yourself, "I have to do this." It wasn't inspired—it felt exhausting.

Choose a specific moment for this to work. Something that actually happened, not something you imagine. How did it feel in your body while you were doing it? Just as in part 1, notice any physical sensations in your muscles, heart rate, or breathing. Notice any feelings. Was there an internal narrative happening in your mind to justify doing it? Was it someone else's request or an internal sense of obligation? Did it feel like it was taking too long or it was pulling energy out of you without giving energy back?

Just notice how you relate to that activity. What's the story you've built around it? How does your body respond when you think about it? Is there tension somewhere—your shoulders, your chest, your jaw? Do you feel heavy, closed, or low on energy?

Ask yourself if you would want to keep doing that activity again and again. Or are you white-knuckling through until it's over with, so you can move on and not think about it anymore? Pay attention to how your body reacts to this experience. Something is different. Be aware of how you feel in your body while you are doing that activity.

When you are finished, open your eyes and move your body again. Shake your arms, stretch your neck, bend your knees—well done.

Inspiration and Have-Tos

We all operate with 2 types of activities. Let's call them high-priority activities, or *inspiration*, and low-priority activities, or *have-tos*. Our brain operates in 2 different ways, depending on which type we're engaging in. Let's imagine 2 columns labeled according to those activities: *inspiration* and *have-tos*.

In the inspiration column you have your highest priorities—the things that have truly mattered most to you over the past few months. These aren't wishful thinking or good intentions, but the activities you consistently focus on and prioritize. And when you engage with them, you feel inspired.

Let's take a general example. Imagine someone whose core inspiration right now is building a great product for their business. Their highest priorities might include:

1. building a great product,

2. implementing a management system,

3. working out, and

4. spending time with their partner.

These reflect their internal hierarchy—ranked from most important to least important. And when they live in alignment with these priorities, something powerful happens: they become present, focused, and disciplined.

That's because acting on your highest priorities activates your forebrain, including the neocortex and the executive center—the most advanced parts of your brain responsible for strategic thinking, vision, planning, and disciplined action.[64]

When these brain regions take control, you gain clarity. You think strategically, stay focused, and follow through. You align your body and mind to do your best work. You enter a state of internal order, which allows you to manifest results more effectively.

In this space, you experience certainty. You don't second-guess yourself. You immediately recognize what aligns with your vision and what doesn't. You stop wasting energy on things that are out of sync.

---

64 The executive center is a functional term referring to brain areas responsible for decision-making, planning, impulse control, and goal-directed behavior. It is located in the prefrontal cortex, which is a part of the neocortex. In summary, the executive center is a function (mostly carried out by the prefrontal cortex). The prefrontal cortex is a part of the neocortex. The neocortex is a part of the forebrain. So, they are nested concepts: forebrain → neocortex → prefrontal cortex (executive center).

And here's an important factor: when you live in your highest priorities, you naturally seek out challenges. You don't attract unnecessary drama because you're not resisting difficulty—you're embracing it. A child who loves video games will naturally pursue the more advanced and challenging levels. They don't want the game to be easier. The same is true for someone who loves going to the gym—they don't complain that exercising is difficult.

Embracing challenge means accepting both the ease and the struggle. It's seeing the beauty in what's hard, not just in what's easy. It's the capacity to hold both the positive and the negative—simultaneously—and move forward. That's the space where true manifestation begins. That's why you have the highest levels of order in your highest priorities.

Now, for the have-tos column, we'll continue with the list we began in the first column. I'll share only a few items here, even though the list could be much longer. The lowest priorities in our example might look like this:

4. spending time with their partner,

5. taking care of the dog,

6. learning about money, and

7. maintaining the garden.

Since the fourth priority—spending time with their partner—sits on the border, we'll include it in both columns. As a borderline priority, it requires conscious effort—intentional time, energy, and attention. Otherwise, their natural focus will gravitate toward the top 3 priorities, leaving this one neglected.

The 2 columns side-by-side will look like this:

INSPIRATION	HAVE-TOS
1. building a great product	4. spending time with their partner
2. implementing a management system	5. taking care of the dog
3. working out	6. learning about money
4. spending time with their partner	7. maintaining the garden

The areas that don't naturally draw your attention belong in the have-tos column. As a result, they often become sources of procrastination. What happens in this space? Instead of focus, you experience distraction. Instead of order, there's chaos. You'll avoid, delay, or rush through these tasks so you can be done with them. You'll feel mentally scattered, uncertain, drained, and you'll begin to doubt yourself.

The more primitive parts of your brain, like the amygdala, take over—triggering survival responses such as fight, flight, or freeze. Here you have the instinct to avoid pain and the impulse to seek pleasure.

This creates a pattern of polarization: you push through the painful task, then reward yourself with something pleasurable. For example, "I learned about money today—that was hard—so now I deserve a sweet." This is how addictions begin: a cycle of energy drain and compensation, simply because you're living outside your true priorities. When you spend much time in these low-priority areas, you can't rely on inspiration. You rely on willpower—which is limited and feels exhausting.

In that state, manifestation becomes difficult. Why? Because your capacity to embrace pain and pleasure is diminished and the higher functions of your brain—like planning, vision, strategy, and disciplined action—are significantly reduced. Functioning in these lower priorities often feels chaotic.

The Brain Was Built for Highest Priorities

There is a myth in personal development literature that our brain's function isn't to make us thrive, but to keep us safe. That's not true, unless we're speaking of the more primitive parts of the brain. The most advanced part of your brain is biologically programmed to help you fulfill your highest priorities. Identity and personal mission are aligned with our highest priority—and when we live from it, we experience a state of flow.

In your highest priorities, you tap into higher energies. It becomes like a perpetual motion machine: you spend energy, but you also generate energy. These activities give back. They recharge you as you engage with them. In your lowest priorities, energy is drained. You're not just tired—you're expending vital life force. You're paying with your days on earth, as living this draining lifestyle can reduce life expectancy. In contrast, when you operate in your highest priorities you're aligned, energized, present, and it adds days to your life.

Here's a crucial point to remember: your highest priority reflects your identity. Imagine 3 women—Maria, Georgia, and Carla—each with different priorities. Maria's top priority is her children—she says "I'm a mother." Georgia lives for sports and calls herself an athlete. Carla, who has no children but is devoted to medicine, says "I'm a doctor." In a crowd, what name would Carla automatically respond to—"mother" or "doctor"?

In your highest priorities, you willingly take on greater challenges. You set bigger goals, even ones that seem impossible to others—because your brain works with you. It gives you access to higher creativity, clearer thinking, and more energy. Rather than relying only on your own resources—you're connecting with something greater. In your lower priorities, it's the opposite. You deplete your energy to get things done, and then you compensate—with a distraction, a treat, or other kind of reward—because those tasks leave you drained.

When you live in your highest priorities, you naturally integrate polarities. You see both sides of situations more quickly. You recognize the deeper order and meaning of your experiences. You're not fighting your mind—you're using it. In your lowest priorities, the polarities persist. It's harder to find balance. Your brain resists integration, and everything feels like an uphill battle.

This is why your brain is designed to manifest in your highest priorities. If we use the 80/20 principle, you'll get 80% of your results from your highest priorities. And you might squeeze out 20% from your lower ones—but through willpower, not inspiration.

Less Have-Tos, More Inspiration

Years ago, I worked with a client named Mia. She owned a catering business that demanded her attention 7 days a week, and she struggled to delegate responsibilities. Her days were filled with lots of *have-tos* and very little inspiration—to the point that it affected her health.

During the weekdays, they primarily delivered lunch subscriptions to companies. Weekends were packed with catering for events, including weddings and corporate gatherings. Mia felt trapped and exhausted because she couldn't entrust anyone else with the operations management.

She had trouble delegating work to others because of a deep mistrust rooted in past experiences, when she had attempted it but people she relied on failed to deliver. These disappointments had left her emotionally scarred, reinforcing the belief that only she could handle the work effectively. Alone and carrying unresolved pain from these past failures, Mia's business—and life—felt like an unrelenting grind.

Mia joined our Inspired Money for Women program, which focuses on balancing feminine and masculine energy within. Exclusively for women, the program's purpose is teaching them to trust in passing things on—essentially, to delegate confidently—and letting others do the work for them. It's about learning to receive more, embracing feminine energy, and allowing masculine energy to take its rightful place. It's a different way of bringing order to different areas of life and achieving inner alignment.

Mia's work ethic was evident from day one of the program. She threw herself into the exercises, diligently dissolving the emotional baggage she carried from her past. This included addressing the disappointments with both men and women who had let her down. She identified the hidden benefits of those experiences, releasing the pain, and seeing these events with a more balanced perspective.

Next, we tackled her belief that only she could do things the "right" way. This mindset created a polarized view: Mia saw herself as very capable and others as quite incapable. With this mindset, why would someone ever delegate? It was a clear example of imbalanced perceptions and missing information that created disorder.

A breakthrough happened for Mia at work while she was in the program. A client requested catering one weekend and Mark, Mia's right-hand colleague, offered to take charge. For the first time, Mia trusted someone else to handle this client. To her surprise, the client agreed to the arrangement without hesitation. This shift wasn't a coincidence. Mia's newfound confidence and internal alignment allowed her to project trust and assurance, which the client sensed.

The catering event went exceptionally well. The client was so impressed that he gave the company a hefty tip, which covered Mark's work bonus. This was a turning point for Mia.

Six months later, Mia handed over operational management to Mark. This allowed her to focus on what was inspiring to her: strategy, branding, and developing new partnerships to expand her market reach. By integrating both sides—benefits and drawbacks—and creating a higher degree of inner order, Mia's external reality transformed faster than she had ever imagined.

Clean the Past to Create Order

To access a new reality, your thoughts and emotions must be aligned with it. That's internal order, or coherence. But if you associate more pain than pleasure with the reality you want to create, you won't be able to access it. This was Mia's case. She claimed she wanted to delegate the operations in her business to someone else, but for years she made excuses like, "Clients refuse to work with anyone else but me," or "No one else knows how to do it," or "This new project is really different—I can't let someone else do it." Any of these sound familiar?

The first step in overcoming this hurdle is to dissolve the negative charge attached to the desired reality. The pain associated with a new reality often stems from unresolved emotional baggage, such as past events perceived as negative. This process involves seeing the hidden order in your experiences, acknowledging both sides, and integrating benefits and drawbacks, pains and pleasures, positives and negatives until each event is neutral.

For example, if you're a woman and during your childhood you saw your father not supporting your mother and your mother struggling on her own, you might develop an internal belief that relationships lead to pain. As a result, you could become overly independent to avoid experiencing the same suffering your mother did. This need for independence can cause its own issues, however. For instance, when it comes to relationships you might subconsciously view a man as someone you need to support, rather than someone who is an equal partner, because of the pattern you've developed of handling things on your own.

Do you like this dynamic? Probably not. But this is how unresolved emotional patterns can play out. Unhealed pain from the past can lead to repeating patterns in relationships. The first step in breaking these patterns is healing those pains and finding hidden order.

Chaos, an Opportunity to Grow

We all go through periods of both chaos and order in our lives. Life events that bring chaos could be a death in the family, a serious diagnosis, an accident, marriage, having a baby, or changing jobs. Any one of these experiences can dramatically change reality, destabilize, stir up questions. What they all have in common is that what once worked no longer does. Even if things appear to function externally, they no longer feel the same internally.

A company also goes through periods of both order and chaos. Events that bring chaos for a company could be reduced performance of a bestselling product, the emergence of a new competitor who changes the market, change in leadership, turnover in personnel, or a shift in technology. Any of these can threaten the business and require adaptation. Again, one thing is certain: what used to work no longer does.

When this happens, there is a hidden meaning I've seen over and over again in my one-on-one work with hundreds of clients. It's like a calling to a higher level of order. The old level of order has reached its potential, and a new one is needed for evolution. The transition is similar to adolescence—often messy, marked by emotional volatility and identity crises. But we forget that during this period, the human body grows the most after infancy.

We tend to label order as positive and chaos as negative. But the truth is, they coexist. At a fundamental level, they are neither good nor bad—both are necessary. You can't build without destruction. Every new structure begins by dismantling what was there before—an old building or a piece of nature. It starts with dust and noise before it becomes beautiful.

A great example of a company that embraced chaos is Meta (formerly Facebook). Between 2009 and 2014, their internal slogan was "Move fast and break things." It's no coincidence that Facebook saw massive innovation and rapid growth during those years. The slogan was misunderstood and criticized by many who viewed chaos as bad and order as good.

The truth is, when a company remains too long at a certain level of order, it stops innovating, becomes rigid, and loses adaptability. On the other hand, staying too long in chaos can quickly lead to decline. It's easier to observe this in companies than in our personal lives, but the principle is the same: we need both order and chaos to grow and stay fit. Maximum growth occurs at the edge between chaos and order.

Antonio's Journey to Building a Green City

Antonio is an amazing landscape designer, a client, and a friend. Two years ago, he participated in our Money Alchemy program with great enthusiasm, and his desire to grow was contagious. During one of the exercises, he entered a space of infinite potential and visualized himself creating a green city, shaped by his unique vision.

Antonio already had a successful business and a great reputation. He had worked on beautiful residential projects and was the go-to landscape designer for the wealthiest individuals in the region. Despite this achievement, however, he felt he had hit a plateau. The projects that came to him felt repetitive, and although he wanted more, he couldn't seem to move beyond his current level.

For 2 years, Antonio wrestled with this feeling of being stuck. He occasionally applied for municipal contracts but only managed to secure small, inconsequential parts of larger projects. It felt like he was scrambling for scraps from a larger table. Although he saw himself capable of much more, he couldn't bridge the gap to reach his higher aspirations. The frustration of being unable to transcend his current level weighed heavily on him.

While working with us in our Money Alchemy program, Antonio experienced a profound transformation. Throughout the exercises, he experienced perfect alignment between himself and his mission. He told me, "Monica, during that exercise, I felt God behind me. It was like God had my back, you know?" This inner alignment is another word for internal order or coherence. He felt like he was already there.

A year later, Antonio called me with exciting news. His vision had materialized. He was commissioned with designing and creating the first green city in his country. This wasn't just a park or a residential area—it was an entire city conceived as a harmonious green landscape, designed according to his vision and adorned with his signature style. The municipality gave him full creative control to bring his dream to life exactly as he had imagined it.

This achievement was monumental. To be handed the reins of an entire city and entrusted with its design was an immense milestone. I am certain this is just the beginning for Antonio. Larger cities will follow, as his vision is genuine and rooted in who he truly is. Dreams manifest when they come from a place of inner order and alignment, not chaos or superficial desire.

David Bohm's Theory of Implicate Order

David Bohm redefined the scientific concept of order like no one else, being described as one of the most significant theoretical physicists of the 20th century. He engaged in deep dialogues with thinkers like Albert Einstein and spiritual teacher Jiddu Krishnamurti, seeking to bridge science and spirituality. In my view, David Bohm carried forward the work of Einstein and Bohr, expanding their debate into new and transformative territory.

Born in 1917, he made significant contributions to plasma physics, the foundations of quantum theory, and the philosophy of science. He is perhaps best known for proposing the theory of the implicate order, a revolutionary view suggesting that the universe is fundamentally interconnected and that what we perceive as separate parts are actually enfolded aspects of a deeper, unified whole.

Imagine 2 vortexes spinning in a river—distinct, swirling patterns that appear separate to the eye. We might point to each and say, "Here is one vortex, and there is another," as if they are independent objects. But in truth, they are not separate things; they are dynamic patterns formed by the same flowing water. Each vortex draws from and contributes to the entire movement of the river. If the flow of the river changes, so do the vortexes—they are inseparable from the whole. In David Bohm's terms, the vortexes represent the explicate order—the visible, seemingly separate forms—while the river itself reflects the implicate order, the deeper, unseen flow that gives rise to those forms. The vortexes may look distinct, but they are enfolded aspects of a single, unified process.

David Bohm's theory of the implicate and explicate order presents a radically different view of reality, emphasizing wholeness over fragmentation. In his view, the explicate order is the world of appearances—the separate, tangible objects and events we observe in space and time. It's the surface layer of reality, much like the images on a screen. Beneath it lies the implicate order, a deeper, unbroken wholeness in which everything is enfolded into everything else. This hidden order is dynamic and generative, constantly unfolding into the explicate and enfolding back again in a continuous process. In this framework, what seems separate and localized is actually an expression of a deeper, interconnected whole.

David Bohm used the metaphor of an ink droplet in glycerin to illustrate the implicate order. When the fluid is slowly rotated, the droplet seems to disappear—its shape enfolded into the liquid. Reversing the motion reveals the droplet again, perfectly intact. This shows how information can be hidden yet preserved, just like the implicate order beneath appearances. What seems to vanish or fragment in the visible world may still exist in a deeper, unified reality— unseen but present, waiting to unfold.

In one-on-one sessions with clients, an FTP specialist who knows the universal laws will begin with a different premise: that there is a hidden order beneath the surface of what we call "problems"—something waiting to be discovered, not fixed. Take procrastination, for example. Most people see it as a flaw, a kind of virus in their system they need to eliminate. But when we look deeper, we often find that procrastination is not random or dysfunctional—it's perfectly coherent with the person's life story and internal logic. In many cases, it was even necessary. This perspective shifts everything. It's not about fighting against behavior but understanding the deeper order it expresses. It's a fundamentally different approach than traditional coaching or psychotherapy.

Question to Apply the Law of Order: *How Did You Co-Create This Situation?*

A few years ago, while I was living in London, I met with a friend of mine, Evelyn, for a coffee. She was going through a painful divorce and working on a plan to move out with her baby. As I handed her the foamy latte she had ordered, she began recounting some events that had unfolded since we'd last seen each other. The dynamic between her and her husband had become unbearable, and she felt it was best for them to get more distance as soon as possible. Evelyn had a clear idea of where she wanted to move—a beautiful compound conveniently located next to her office.

Evelyn already knew that Henry, a family friend, owned an unoccupied rental apartment in that compound. Excited by the opportunity, she reached out to him to inquire about it. Henry confirmed that the apartment was indeed available,

THE 7 UNIVERSAL LAWS

and while he didn't offer her a "friends and family discount," Evelyn agreed to pay the market price for the convenience of the location. As a mother of a young child, time was precious, and being within a 5-minute walk from her office was ideal.

Two days later, however, Henry called Evelyn with disappointing news. He told her he couldn't rent the apartment to her anymore because he had spoken with her husband, who disapproved of the arrangement. Henry explained that he didn't want to jeopardize his business relationship with her husband or his personal relationship with her. Evelyn was understandably upset. "Don't worry, our relationship can't be affected," she said bitterly, "it doesn't exist anymore."

As Evelyn recounted this to me, I was immediately outraged. My first thoughts were, "How ridiculously foolish is that husband of hers? This decision affects his own child too. How could he do this?" I felt similarly about Henry. "Is he out of his mind?" I thought. "It's not like he's offering her any special treatment or discount. Why not treat her like any other client?"

Then I paused as my thoughts spiraled in conflicting directions. According to the universal laws, Evelyn couldn't be merely a passive victim in this situation. Was there something deeper at play here? I wrestled with my own curiosity, trying to reconcile the surface-level unfairness with the hidden order. I asked her, "Can I ask you a weird question? You might not like it." She laughed, knowing I had a knack for asking unconventional questions, and gave me the go-ahead to continue.

"How did you co-create this situation?" I asked. She looked puzzled. "What do you mean I co-created it? This is just unfair, and they are clearly in the wrong." Usually, I don't leave a question without a real answer, but this time I did. Probably because it was a casual conversation over coffee. So I didn't insist, but hugged her goodbye and invited her to sit with the question.

Two days later, Evelyn called me, her voice upbeat. She had found another apartment in the same compound. This one was on the ground floor, and she was thrilled about it. I asked her to compare the first apartment with this one. That's when she revealed something she hadn't mentioned before. "The first apartment was on the fourth floor," she said, "and there was no elevator. You know, I'm not in great shape, and with a baby, it would have been so hard to carry groceries and everything else up those stairs."

At that moment, the situation clicked for both of us. I asked, "Do you see now how you co-created this?" Evelyn paused and then laughed. "Definitely. I was dreading the idea of climbing those stairs every day. I had already imagined how exhausting it would be, especially with groceries and a baby. It terrified me."

It became clear that Evelyn wasn't a victim in this story. She was a powerful creator, manifesting exactly what she truly needed. All of a sudden, both men—Henry and her husband—didn't look like the oppressors anymore, but like 2 accomplices who helped Evelyn get what she really wanted. The new apartment not only had more space and a kind landlord, but it also included an empty room she could use for storage. On top of everything, it was on the ground floor, eliminating her fear of daily stair-climbing.

This experience was an important reminder: we often see ourselves as victims of circumstance when we are actually active participants in creating our own reality. Where we perceive chaos, there is often a hidden order we simply haven't recognized yet. Take your time to discover it.

The next time you find yourself in a situation where something feels like it's happening to you, take a step back and ask: "How did I co-create this?" and "If this problem were actually the solution, what might it be a solution for?" You may uncover powerful insights you hadn't seen before.

Sacred Contracts

Note: This section presents personal belief and there is no scientific support for it. You have every right to disagree with me and disregard this, if you want. Yet many people have told me that this concept redefined how they approached life.

Another great mentor of mine, Caroline Myss, a spiritual teacher and medical intuitive, who worked extensively with Harvard professor and neurologist Dr. Norm Shealy, published the book *Sacred Contracts: Awakening Your Divine Potential* in 2001. While I don't fully agree with everything she says, the idea of sacred contracts could hold some truth. Sacred contracts are spiritual agreements that she believes are formed before birth, in what she describes as the "divine realm." These contracts are made with the divine and with the other souls who will play significant roles in our lives.

Imagine this: before birth, your soul carefully chooses the exact context and circumstances it will incarnate into. It selects a family—a traditional one, a single mother, or even parents who might reject the child. It picks the childhood experiences, the people it will form relationships with, whether it will marry or remain single, and all the events that will shape its journey, right up to the form of its physical death.

I know this might sound far-fetched, but before you dismiss the idea entirely, consider how you play games on your computer or phone. First, you select a character for yourself. Now imagine your soul as the player and the character as your human form. You decide whether your character will be male or female, what kind of outfit it will wear, what weapons or skills it will have, and then you dive into the game. Since you've played the game before, this time you start with a sense of purpose—you already know where you want to go, what you want to build, and who you want to battle along the way. When you get tired or you reach the end, you might decide to add a dramatic twist: perhaps you let the big monster kill you, or you leap off a cliff and you die that way and exit the game. When you think about it like this, it doesn't seem quite so crazy, does it?

The idea behind sacred contracts is not new. Nearly 2,400 years ago, Plato discussed it in book X of *The Republic*, as a conclusion to his famous work. In "The Myth of Er," souls are judged after death and are then given the opportunity to choose their next life. Plato emphasizes that this is neither random nor predetermined. Instead, it is presented as a highly individual choice, where souls can select from various lives, each with its own rewards, challenges, and opportunities. The idea that souls are responsible for their choices implies that they have inherent freedom in shaping their destiny. This concept has echoed through spiritual and philosophical writings for over 2000 years. Helena

Blavatsky and Annie Besant, key figures in the theosophical movement, brought renewed attention to the soul's journey and pre-birth agreements during the 19th century.

The primary purpose of sacred contracts is spiritual growth and evolution. Caroline Myss teaches that these contracts exist to help souls learn specific lessons, develop particular strengths, overcome challenges, and ultimately fulfill their divine purpose. They represent a blueprint for our spiritual journey in this lifetime.

For example, a woman may have a sacred contract as a teacher, agreeing before birth to guide others in discovering their potential and wisdom. Her life is marked by early struggles with self-doubt and lack of confidence—forcing her to learn, accumulate knowledge, and practice with many people in order to get certainty. These experiences prepare her to assist others through similar challenges. She feels an inner pull toward teaching, first in traditional education and later as a mentor in personal development. Through her work, she not only educates people but also fulfills her soul's purpose of sharing knowledge and inspiring growth, transforming her own pain into a source of healing and wisdom for others.

Whether or not you agree with the idea of sacred contracts, it undeniably represents a profound paradigm shift. Imagine what could be possible for an individual who embraces this perspective—taking complete responsibility for their life. Consider the impact it would have to believe that we chose the family we were born into, the hardships we would face in this life, the education we would receive, the illnesses we would endure, and even the friends and foes we would encounter throughout life.

This perspective doesn't negate free will. Like in a game, when you choose a character, you still make decisions along the way. But *you* chose to play that particular game. Nobody forced you. *You* chose to be born into wealth or poverty, health or illness, with more or less education.

Now ask yourself: What would be possible if you truly believed you had made these choices? What if, where others see chaos, there is a hidden order waiting to be discovered? How would your story change if you saw yourself not as a subject of fate, but as the author of your own experience?

Summary

Your capacity to manifest results, solve problems, or lead others depends entirely on the level of internal order you maintain. And here's the core idea: you have the most order in your highest priorities, and that's exactly where your mind seeks to grow and create more. In those areas, your mind naturally embraces pain and pleasure, positives and negatives. You connect the dots, anticipate outcomes, and see things as part of an integrated system. That's why results flow more easily there.

But in your lower priorities, you crave only the upside and reject the downside. That rejection creates distortion. It blocks clarity. It creates disorder—not because something is wrong, but because you're missing information. Disorder, as Claude Shannon pointed out, is a result of missing information. And missing information keeps you stuck. That's why true transformation starts by seeing more of the whole. The more of the whole you can see—the clearer your vision, the more grounded your choices, and the more stable your results.

Sometimes the very reason you can't live in alignment with your highest priorities is because unresolved pain from the past is running the show, keeping you in the same patterns. Painful memories—especially those charged with guilt, fear, or rejection—can silently dictate your decisions, pulling you away from what truly matters to you. Until those emotional imprints are seen, felt, and cleared, they create resistance. You may say you want success, love, or freedom, but if part of you still associates those things with pain, your mind will hold back to protect you. Clearing those memories is about dissolving the emotional weight so you can move forward without internal conflict.

This chapter shows that order is not just a mental concept—it's a lived experience. It is the principle that guides your evolution. And it's contextual. You don't need to have it everywhere—but where you do have it, you lead. The key to living a fulfilling life is to live in alignment with your highest priorities.

Practical Application

You've probably already asked yourself how to put this into practice and what your highest priorities are. Here are 2 ways to support you in taking the first steps and identifying the true hierarchy of your priorities.

1. Identify Your Highest Priorities on Your Own

Access the link below to watch a video that guides you through identifying your highest priorities. The beauty of a video is that you can pause or repeat as often as you like. Watch for our app on this topic soon.

InspiredLifeCircle.com/video-priorities

2. Identify Your Highest Priorities, with Support

One of our specialists can offer deeper insights based on their experience and expertise, giving you confidence that you've identified them correctly.

InspiredLifeCircle.com/identify-priorities-meeting

Knowing your highest priorities is crucial because they're the areas where you naturally have the most internal order, clarity, and energy. In these areas, you're willing to embrace both pain and pleasure. This internal order enables more effective manifestation, better decision-making, and lasting results.

CHAPTER 9

THE LAW OF FRACTALS

If you cannot do great things yourself, remember that you may do small things in a great way.

— Napoleon Hill

The Fractal of a Friendship

A few years ago, I went out for dinner in London with my teenage daughter, Elena, and her new friend, Katty. We were exchanging casual conversation when Katty shared something peculiar about her eating habits.

"The way I deal with food is simple," she said. "I eat the exact same thing for every meal—breakfast, lunch, dinner—until I can't stand it anymore. Then, when I get so sick of it that it makes me throw up, I stop eating that food altogether and won't touch it for a long time."

I found this habit fascinating. It wasn't just quirky—it was a perfect example of a pattern that would show up in other areas of life. "A fractal," I thought to myself. Later, when Katty excused herself to the bathroom, I leaned over to Elena. "Can you guess how your friendship with Katty will end?"

Elena raised an eyebrow. "No," she said. "But I'm curious to hear what you think."

"Well," I began, "I could see the 2 of you becoming very close, and then one day, the friendship might just end. Very suddenly."

Elena's eyes widened in disbelief. "That sounds horrible, Mom! I don't think that's what's going to happen."

I smiled. "Well, let's hope I'm wrong," I said, "but I wouldn't bet on it!"

When Katty returned, I decided to probe a little further. "Katty," I asked, "have you ever really gotten into something and then suddenly stopped?"

"Oh, totally," she said. "I'm an artist, and I once decided to focus entirely on oil painting. I threw myself into it, painting obsessively, and then one day, I just gave up. Completely." She continued, upbeat, "Then I moved on to pottery. I got really into clay modeling. And, same thing—after a while, I just quit."

The pattern was clear. I glanced at Elena and made a subtle gesture, as if to say, "See?" She shrugged.

A year later, exactly as I had predicted, their friendship abruptly ended. One day, they were inseparable; the next, they weren't speaking at all. Katty's tendency to immerse herself fully in something and then abandon it had played out in her friendship with Elena.

But it didn't stop there. A little while later, Katty's relationship with her boyfriend followed the same trajectory. They had been incredibly close, and then suddenly it was over.

Reflecting on this, you may notice that the specifics—whether it was food, art, or relationships—didn't matter. It wasn't about the content; it was about the process. Katty's pattern of thinking, feeling, and behaving created the same outcomes across different areas of her life. The process was consistent, regardless of the content.

This story serves as a reminder that understanding someone's patterns can offer profound insights into how they navigate the world. It's a fractal—a small, repeating pattern that mirrors itself on a larger scale. And once you see it, you can't unsee it.

Definition of the Law of Fractals

The law of fractals states that

"the way you do one thing is the way you do everything."[65]

This principle emerges from chaos theory, which examines seemingly random structures which, upon closer inspection, reveal underlying order. Chaos often appears disorganized, yet within it, certain repetitive sequences form patterns. These recurring sequences create structure within the chaos.

---

65 Zen proverb, popularized by Zen teacher and author Cheri Huber, who used it as the title and central theme of her 1988 workbook, *How You Do Anything Is How You Do Everything: A Workbook.*

One example is the leaf. The back of a leaf demonstrates fractal properties because its vein structure mirrors the hierarchical pattern of the leaf itself and the broader tree. Just as a tree's branches subdivide into smaller branches and twigs, forming self-similar patterns at different scales, the leaf's primary vein branches into secondary and tertiary veins, mimicking this organization. This self-repeating pattern reflects the tree's growth strategy, optimizing nutrient transport and structural support at every level—from the whole tree to individual leaves. Thus, the back of a leaf is a fractal microcosm of the leaf's structure and, in turn, the tree's overall form.

The terms *fractal*, *pattern*, and *archetype* are used inter-changeably in this chapter. While there are differences between them, these distinctions aren't essential for what we're exploring here.

Practically speaking, the law of fractals brings order to chaos by revealing small patterns within a larger image. According to this law, each small fractal is a perfect repre-sentation of the whole. A common example is the seashell spiral, like that of a nautilus. Its shape follows a logarithmic spiral, a self-similar pattern that repeats at different scales. As the shell grows, each new section retains the same proportions as the previous one, creating a consistent and predictable pattern.

This concept forms the basis of the saying: "The way you do one thing is the way you do everything." Whatever sequence you take from someone's life—whether it's a moment, a day, a week, a year, or 10 years—that sequence reproduces and reflects the whole.

Look at Katty, for instance. Her food fractal followed a pattern of complete immersion—an all-or-nothing approach. Once she grew tired of a certain food, she would abruptly abandon it, with no gradual transition. The same pattern shows up in her friendships. She forms deep, intense connections, but when the dynamic changes or she feels "saturated," the relationship ends just as abruptly. This fractal reflects a consistent cycle of total involvement followed by abrupt detachment, repeating across various aspects of her life.

A fractal, in essence, is a stream of thoughts, emotions, and behaviors that lead to a predictable outcome. Regardless of content, the same fractals manifest in various aspects of life: money, relationships, business, and interactions with colleagues, among others. In practical terms, a fractal represents a process in which thoughts, emotions, and behaviors are interconnected. This process guarantees specific results or outcomes, repeating across different domains of life.

The reason a fractal is important is because it defines what's possible—and what's not—within it. If you think of a fractal as a frequency or an archetype, it becomes easier to see: certain outcomes can only be achieved within certain archetypes, while others are naturally out of reach. For example, the archetype of a warrior doesn't align with delivering an exceptional customer experience—that requires empathy, presence, and care. Likewise, the archetype of a lover doesn't fit with successful trading on Wall Street.

So when you're aiming for a specific result, it's much easier if your goal aligns with your fractal, or if you align your fractal with the goal. If it doesn't, you'll likely meet resistance and struggle along the way. In this chapter, you'll find valuable insights on how to work with fractals to your advantage and avoid going against them.

My "Working Hard" Fractal

For as far back as I can remember, my life was shaped by the "working hard" fractal. The "working hard" pattern operates like an internal operating system for the brain, aligning emotions, thoughts, and actions in a way that reinforces the belief that constant effort is the only way to achieve anything.

This "working hard" pattern took form early on in my life. As a child, I watched my mother work tirelessly. Everything seemed hard for her—earning money, completing tasks, managing the household. Money, in particular, was a constant source of difficulty. During holidays, she worked herself to exhaustion. By the time Christmas dinner was ready, she was completely drained. She couldn't take care of herself because she felt obligated to meet everyone's needs. She often went above and beyond, even when it meant doing more than was necessary, and felt unsupported—especially when my dad wouldn't help with simple chores. That was the model I grew up with, and it left a lasting impression.

Then there was the way hard work was valued. When I was a kid, if I did nothing, I was scolded. But if I worked hard—even if that meant staying up until midnight finishing homework—I was praised. My math teacher piled on homework so relentlessly that my evenings were swallowed by numbers and equations. I'd come home, eat, and then lose myself in math until midnight. Other subjects hardly mattered because my energy was devoted to math. My late-night efforts were celebrated by both my teacher and my parents, reinforcing that "working hard" was the only way.

But here's the twist: this pattern only works until it doesn't. When a fractal depletes its potential for you, you will see clear signs that it's no longer effective. One day, about 10 years ago, I simply couldn't get out of bed. It wasn't depression—it was pure exhaustion. I had been running on this "working hard" mode in multiple areas of my life until I burned out. My body, overwhelmed by the strain, refused to keep up with my relentless mind.

Imagine waking up with your mind buzzing while your body feels completely disconnected and refuses to comply. In hindsight, I'm grateful for that wake-up call—even though it came in the form of burnout.

That moment forced me to seriously reevaluate my life. I began the work of reorganizing and transforming this pattern. I realized that my way of working wasn't sustainable, and it certainly wasn't leading me to the results I truly desired. This transformation wasn't just important—it was profound. I changed how I approached my work. As a result, I now have the freedom to choose how much I work and what I focus on. I gravitate toward tasks that energize and inspire me, and I steer clear of those that drain me.

This transformation required deep inner work. Up until a few years ago, I operated under the belief that I had to do everything, no matter the cost. Many of you who resonate with the "working hard" fractal can likely confirm that it leads to burnout and chronic exhaustion. It brings you to a point where you question, "Why am I struggling so much? Is this really worth it?"

In this chapter, we're going to explore fractals: what they are, what they mean, and how they shape our lives. By the end of this chapter, you'll have a tool you can use to start transforming your fractal today. While the full process involves interconnected elements from other universal laws (which we cover in more advanced courses), this chapter will give you a powerful starting point.

The Science of Fractals

The study of fractals is a relatively recent development. What was once thought to be completely random has, in recent decades, been revealed by modern science to contain a hidden order. For instance, fractal geometry, a distinct branch of mathematics, is considered to have been formally born in 1975, when Benoit B. Mandelbrot introduced the term *fractal* in his paper "Fractal Objects: Form, Chance, and Dimension."[66]

Before Mandelbrot's work, irregular structures in nature—such as coastlines, clouds, and mountains—were often considered entirely chaotic and unpredictable. But with the publication of his groundbreaking book in 1982, *The Fractal Geometry of Nature*, Mandelbrot revealed that these seemingly erratic forms actually possess a hidden order. He demonstrated that fractals provide a mathematical framework for understanding and visualizing this hidden order, uncovering patterns that humanity had long overlooked.

---

66 Benoit B. Mandelbrot, "Fractal Objects: Form, Chance, and Dimension," *Science* 187, no. 4175 (1975): 382–389.

Another study conducted in the 1990s, associated with Harvard Medical School and led by Ary L. Goldberger and his colleagues, revealed that healthy heart rhythms display fractal-like behavior.[67] These findings challenged earlier views of heart function and opened new doors for diagnosing and treating cardiovascular diseases. Again, what was once believed to be chaotic has now been discovered to possess a hidden order.

Goldberger's team demonstrated that fractal patterns arise from the interplay of multiple physiological control mechanisms, such as the autonomic nervous system. Healthy hearts show complex variability, which is indicative of the body's ability to respond to changing conditions. In contrast, reduced fractal complexity in heart rate patterns was associated with aging, disease, or an increased risk of sudden cardiac events. These insights were particularly groundbreaking because they revealed that deviations from fractal patterns could serve as early markers for conditions like heart failure or arrhythmia.

The study highlighted the importance of viewing biological systems through the lens of fractal mathematics. This approach not only provided new diagnostic tools but also offered a deeper understanding of the interplay between structure and function in living systems. By recognizing fractal patterns in heart rhythms, researchers were able to bridge mathematics, biology, and medicine—demonstrating the profound utility of fractal analysis in improving human health.

---

67 Ary L. Goldberger, David R. Rigney, and Bruce J. West. "Chaos and Fractals in Human Physiology." *Scientific American* 262, no. 2 (1990): 42–49.

In the realm of psychology, Carl Jung started to write about patterns in the 1910s, and he called them *archetypes.* He believed that these archetypes are part of what he called the *collective unconscious*—a deep layer of the mind shared by all humans, filled with inherited memories and instincts.[68] Archetypes aren't specific images, but more like fundamental templates or blueprints. For example, the idea of the hero, mother, lover, or wise old man are archetypes that appear in myths, dreams, and stories all over the world.

Jung argued that these archetypes influence our personalities and the way we see the world, often without us realizing it. They help explain why people from different places tell similar kinds of stories or react to situations in familiar ways. For instance, the hero archetype often represents personal growth, facing challenges, and overcoming obstacles, which are themes we see in countless stories from ancient myths to modern movies.

Later, in the 1950s, Joseph Campbell expanded on Jung's work and wrote about archetypes extensively in his seminal book, *The Hero with a Thousand Faces*. Campbell synthesized insights from mythology, anthropology, psychology, and literature to explore the universal patterns of storytelling and the human experience.

Unlocking Growth with the Law of Fractals

The law of fractals is a profound concept that can significantly influence your growth and progress. Here's why it matters and how you can harness its potential to your advantage.

68 C. G. Jung, *The Archetypes and the Collective Unconscious*, trans. R. F. C. Hull (Princeton University Press, 1959). Original work published 1934.

Understanding Fractals and Their Potential

Recognize a specific fractal in your life—a recurring pattern of thought or behavior. Each fractal is like a frequency carrying a certain potential, enabling you to progress from one level to another. For example, the "working hard" fractal helped you evolve from earning $10 per hour to $100 per hour. But since you only have 24 hours in a day, you realize you don't have additional time or energy to work even harder. Therefore, you need a different approach. What could that be?

The Role of Fractals in Growth

Fractals are important because each one operates at a specific frequency and has its own limits. While a fractal can be instrumental in achieving certain milestones, it may later hinder your progress. Let's continue with the "working hard" fractal. This archetype is invaluable when launching a business or achieving early-stage goals. But maintaining this pattern for 20 or 30 years isn't sustainable. Over time, it can lead to burnout and stagnation, as you've likely observed in others.

Expanding Your Fractals

To continue growing, it's wise to recognize when a fractal has fulfilled its purpose and transition to a new one. Here's how:

1. Recognize the Limitation

When you're stuck at a plateau, such as $100 per hour, it's a clear indication that your current fractal has reached its potential.

2. Adopt a New Fractal

Think of it as accessing a new frequency, with a different potential. For example, Fractal B might replace Fractal A and take you from $100 to $300 per hour.

3. Repeat the Process

Once Fractal B reaches its limit, transition to Fractal C, which could take you from $300 to $600 per hour. This is meaningful work because it prioritizes inner transformation as the pathway to external results.

Key Principles to Remember

1. Set Realistic Goals Within Your Current Fractal

While operating within Fractal A, avoid setting objectives that belong to Fractal C. It's unrealistic and counterproductive to aim for $600 outcomes while your current fractal only supports growth up to $100.

2. Value Each Fractal for Its Contribution

Fractals are neither good nor bad. Fractal A, for example, was perfect for taking you from $10 to $100. Appreciate it for what it has achieved, even as you prepare to transition to the next phase.

By understanding and applying the law of fractals, you can navigate growth with clarity and purpose, ensuring each stage of your journey builds on the last.

First Question to Apply the Law of Fractals: *How Have You Co-Created This Situation?*

A few years ago, I worked with a client named Grace, a small business owner, in a predicament that seemed impossible to resolve. Quick on her feet, with a bubbly personality and can-do attitude, she was the kind of person who rolled up her sleeves and got things done. At one point, however, she realized that stepping back was necessary for her business to grow, so she delegated its operational management. That's when she hired Dan, a meticulous manager, and went to great lengths to ensure his success.

Grace later outlined her efforts in detail. "I gave him a lot of authority, supported him in every way I could, and even made compromises," she explained. "I changed some of the company's rules and procedures just to accommodate him."

Her company had a small, entrepreneurial culture where quick action and collaboration were key. But after a few months, a stark disconnect became apparent. Grace noticed that Dan's behavior clashed significantly with her team's dynamic. Dan's approach was procedural, almost bureaucratic. "It was like he thought he was working for an old government institution," Grace said, exasperated. "He was reactive instead of proactive. It just didn't fit."

When Grace decided to let Dan go, he resisted. "You can't just terminate my contract," he said, presenting legal documents. He even went as far as threatening legal action because the law in their country favored his situation. To make matters worse, Dan's presence created chaos within the company. He disregarded her instructions, lost clients, and maintained a hostile attitude. Grace's frustration was evident. "It's been 3 months of constant problems and uncertainty," she told me.

When Grace sought my support, I asked her a direct question: "How do you think you co-created this situation?" She frowned, her eyes narrowing. "Monica, I honestly don't see how I could have co-created this situation," she replied.

We dove deeper, and in that session we uncovered something critical. Dan's demeanor mirrored the behavior of Grace's father, a man she admired and whose approval she had often sought after. Grace described her father as a career military man who was precise, well-organized, and adhered strictly to rules and laws. Dan's rigid and disciplined nature was a near-perfect reflection of these qualities.

I explained, "Grace, if you don't address your personal patterns, or fractals, they will inevitably show up in your business. You admire your father, so it's natural that you recreated this dynamic here."

Grace's fractal was to have strong, structured men in her life to whom she could prove her worth—exactly as she wanted to prove her worth in relation to her father. When she met her husband, he was in the army too. So we're talking about the same type of haircut, the same strictness about rules and their adherence, and the same solid, dependable structure.

On a subconscious level, she had chosen a man like her father, hoping that through her husband, she could demonstrate her value. Now, with Dan, she was repeating the same pattern—seeking the validation she had longed for from her father, which is why she kept attracting men like him into her life. At the same time, through this fractal, she was also recreating a man she could rely on, like her father.

She sat there for a moment, absorbed in the realization that had just settled over her. "I've never thought about it like that," she said, her eyes lighting up with new understanding. "But it makes so much sense now."

Over the course of 2 sessions, we worked on balancing her perceptions that she did not get appreciation from her dad, taking him off the pedestal and arriving at a place where she could hold him in gratitude. As Grace began to address these unresolved dynamics, something unexpected happened. Dan approached her and said: "I've decided this isn't the right fit for me." Without further conflict or legal disputes, he resigned.

"Wow, it felt like the issue resolved itself," she shared with me with satisfaction. She didn't change her behavior, didn't hire lawyers, and didn't get into conflicts. She simply did the inner work, balancing the root cause. What Grace couldn't resolve in 2 months, she managed to shift in just 2 hours of inner work.

By addressing her own unresolved dynamics that were the root cause of her fractal, the external problem resolved itself effortlessly. Her experience highlighted a powerful truth: when you address your inner patterns, the external dynamics often shift in remarkable ways. Grace's story is a powerful example of how fractals can change when a new level of internal order is established.

The 2 Layers of Co-Creation: Behavior and Purpose

The question "How did you co-create this reality?" has 2 layers.

For the first layer, ask yourself: "In what ways did my thoughts, emotions, and behaviors co-create this reality?"

For example, you co-created this reality by not setting firm boundaries. In this case, we know exactly what we need to work on. And we'll ask questions like "What benefits do others get when you set firm boundaries? What benefits do *you* get when you set firm boundaries? What are the drawbacks when you don't set firm boundaries?" and so on. These questions are meant to unlock the mind so it wants to set firm boundaries.

For the second layer, ask yourself: "What is the higher purpose for which I co-created this situation?"

Here's a subtle nuance that makes a difference: the answer you give should already be resolved at the moment of perception. For example, if your answer is "to learn how to…" or "to discover how…," these types of responses suggest you're not there yet—you haven't integrated the lesson, you haven't found the solution. But if your answer is already manifested in the present moment of perception, then cause and effect are simultaneously present—they compensate and balance each other.

Fractals in Business

A fractal is a process, not a single event, and it doesn't *have* to have a name. In the end, it's just a sequence of steps leading to a predictable result. It doesn't necessarily need an external label. You can give it a name if you want, but ultimately, the name itself doesn't matter.

What matters is that everything you do aligns with that fractal—you can't act outside of it even if you wanted to. A great analogy to understand the fractal is a computer's operating system. The operating system allows you to do certain things and prevents you from doing others. To change the operating system, you either need a different system (another fractal) or you need to modify the source code (the root cause).

In the business realm, just like in other areas of life, certain fractals emerge that are common among entrepreneurs. We also call them archetypes or patterns. These patterns influence behavior, decision-making, and ultimately the trajectory of the business. Here are some examples:

The Directive Pattern

This pattern is characterized by a strong focus on control. Entrepreneurs or leaders who exhibit this behavior and the emotional aspect of it prefer everything to be exact, procedural, and orderly. They ensure that calculations are precise, that everyone knows their roles, and that well-organized systems are implemented. While this approach can create stability and efficiency, it may also stifle flexibility and innovation in certain contexts.

The Know-It-All Pattern

Entrepreneurs displaying this pattern feel the need to personally excel in every aspect of their business—marketing, sales, product development, delivery, etc. They project an image of being the expert in all domains. While this can cultivate a certain level of confidence and authority, it may hinder delegation, collaboration, and the development of specialized expertise within the team.

The Technician Pattern

This pattern is seen in individuals who view their business as a masterpiece, focusing deeply on their expertise in one particular area. Their businesses often reflect their personal touch or technical skill. While this can result in high-quality offerings, it may limit scalability and the ability to adapt to broader strategic needs.

The Parent Pattern

Leaders with this pattern see themselves as protectors and mentors to their employees, fostering a nurturing and supportive environment. While this can build loyalty and a close-knit culture, it may lead to micromanagement, over-involvement, or dependency, potentially hindering employees' autonomy and growth.

The Competitive Pattern

In this scenario, everything is framed as a win or loss. Cooperation is minimal, and the language used often reflects this mindset, with expressions like "find their Achilles' heel," "crush the competition," and "make a killing." This approach can drive short-term results but may create a high-stress, adversarial environment that limits collaboration and long-term sustainability.

The Relational Pattern

This pattern prioritizes harmony and relationships. Entrepreneurs with this mindset struggle to set boundaries and they avoid saying no to clients and employees, often overworking themselves so no one gets upset. They value employee well-being and emphasize creating a supportive, collaborative workplace. While this encourages a positive work culture, it often comes at the expense of lower business results and small profits.

The patterns described above are just a few examples of the countless fractals that shape business behavior. By identifying and understanding these sequences of behaviors, entrepreneurs can become aware of what is going on in their mind and make conscious choices to overcome them and reach new heights.

These patterns are neither inherently good nor bad. Each has contexts where it is effective and contexts where it becomes limiting. When a business or individual feels stuck, it often means the current pattern has exhausted its potential and no longer serves the situation. Recognizing and shifting these patterns can unlock new possibilities and growth, but it can be one of the most challenging transformations you'll experience.

Second Question to Apply the Law of Fractals: *What's the Name of the Game You're Playing?*

A few years ago, an FTP specialist and a colleague of mine worked with an entrepreneur, who we'll call Jack. Jack went to her with a problem: his marketing department wasn't delivering the results he needed, and he was feeling the weight of it all. Jack understood that his internal reality shaped his external outcomes, and he was open to working on himself before making any external changes.

"I'm the one who gets results," Jack explained. "The weight of the entire company rests on my shoulders. I'm the one signing contracts, handling PR, and taking initiatives. We only see results when I take care of everything," he said, with a tinge of pride in his voice. During their first conversation, my colleague asked him directly, "Jack, what's the game you're playing in your company?"

He looked at my colleague, puzzled. "What do you mean, game? I'm not playing any games here." She smiled and explained. "Jack, what's the pattern you're operating out of? Or in other words, what game are you playing in relation to your employees?"

He stared at her blankly, not responding. A blank stare from someone often signals that you've posed exactly the right question. "The game you're playing, Jack, is called 'Know-It-All.' You're operating from a pattern where you see yourself as the smartest person in the room. When entrepreneurs play this game, their teams often compensate by showing incompetence."

Jack looked down for a moment, considering her words. He took a deep breath and let it out slowly. "You're right. And I just realized that I'm tired of being the smartest person in the room, but I don't know how to change it. Whatever I do, I recreate the same dynamic."

My colleague nodded. "That's exactly why we'll work on changing the pattern." She decided to start by applying the law of duality. "Give me specific examples of times when you didn't achieve results in marketing," my colleague asked him. "Think of a moment when your sales efforts didn't work." Jack struggled at first, but my colleague encouraged him to keep going.

Slowly, Jack began recalling instances where he had failed: "Pricing mistakes...losing major contracts...being too arrogant and demanding too much, which led to lost deals..." and on it went. By the end of the exercise, Jack had listed more than 70 examples of things that hadn't worked out. "I see it now," Jack said, reflecting on his list. "I wasn't always the smartest person in the room. I've made both smart and foolish decisions in my area of expertise."

Once Jack had that realization, my colleague flipped the perspective. "Now let's find at least 50 moments when your marketing department had achievements," she suggested. Jack thought for a moment, then started to list them: "Creating ads with impact...launching a successful event... performing well with smaller product campaigns..." He was starting to see his team in a new light.

The following week, something extraordinary happened. The marketing department delivered the best results they had ever achieved, surpassing anything Jack had done on his own in the previous quarter. Jack was amazed. "I can't believe it. It looks like I created the space for them to operate at their full potential."

Change is effective and quick if you address the root cause of the problem. That shift in Jack's thinking not only trans-formed his leadership style, but it also demonstrated the profound impact of internal changes leading to remarkable external outcomes. By stepping out of his limiting pattern, Jack allowed his team to thrive.

How Patterns or Fractals are Formed

First, you're born into a fractal, inherited from your parents or caregivers. It starts with mimicking behaviors, rules, and patterns you observe in early childhood. Take the idea of "working hard." If you grew up watching a parent who pushed themselves relentlessly, you might carry that same orientation into your own life. It can shape how you study, how you navigate relationships, and how you respond to challenges—working hard becomes your default mode. These patterns are learned behaviors, passed down across generations.

Fractals are fascinating because they contain the seed for anything and everything within you. Your brain prioritizes certain patterns based on experiences, deeming them more efficient, safer, or "the best way" to navigate the world. While this might seem adaptive, it's also limiting. It constrains you to specific ways of being, overshadowing the vast potential you possess.

There are 3 main ways patterns or fractals are formed:

1. Inheritance from Parents

Fractals are most commonly formed by learning and inheriting patterns from your parents. This often involves mirroring their behaviors, rules, or attitudes. For example, children with critical parents may develop perfectionist tendencies as a way to cope or seek validation. This fractal manifests as a drive for flawlessness and can become deeply ingrained, influencing multiple areas of life.

2. Opposition to Parental Patterns

Another way fractals form is in opposition to parental behaviors. For instance, if a child grows up with an absent father, they might internalize a promise to be the opposite—a present and attentive parent. This reactionary type of response is a powerful force in shaping patterns.

3. Personal Experience

Fractals can also emerge from personal experiences. For example, a person who was loyal to a partner but experienced so-called betrayal might form a pattern of avoiding commitment or faithfulness. This coping mechanism becomes their new fractal, shaped by the false lessons they've drawn from their experiences.

These pathways to forming fractals—inheritance, opposition, and personal experience—are not mutually exclusive. They often intertwine, resulting in unique, individualized patterns for each person. While these patterns guide behavior, recognizing and understanding them are the first steps toward breaking free from their constraints and realizing the full spectrum of possibilities within yourself.

Grandma's Cooking Secret[69]

Once upon a time, there was a young couple who had just gotten married and moved into their first home. One Sunday

---

69 This anecdote has roots in Jewish folklore and is used as a teaching tool to emphasize understanding the reasons behind traditions rather than following them blindly. It appears in various forms across books, articles,

afternoon, the husband walked into the kitchen and saw his wife preparing a roast for dinner.

As he watched her, he noticed something odd. Before placing the roast in the pan, she took a sharp knife and carefully cut off both ends of the meat. He raised an eyebrow and asked, "Why do you cut off the ends of the roast? That's the best part."

She replied, "That's how it's done. That's how my mother always made it."

The husband was curious. The answer didn't sit right with him, so the next time they visited his in-laws, he brought it up. He turned to his wife's mother and asked, "Why do you cut the ends off the roast before cooking it?"

She nodded and said, "Oh, that's just how my mother did it. It's the way I was taught."

Still not satisfied, he waited until the next family gathering, where he found the grandmother sitting peacefully in the garden. Sitting beside her, he recounted what he'd seen and asked, "Grandma, why did you always cut the ends off the roast before putting it in the oven?"

The grandmother burst into laughter.

"Oh my goodness," she said, "Are you all still doing that? I only cut the ends off because back in those days, my roasting pan was too small. That was the only way I could make the meat fit!"

The husband chuckled, shaking his head in disbelief.

---

and online discussions dating back to at least the 1950s, with adaptations in different cultures (e.g., sometimes it's a fish or turkey instead of a roast).

Two generations had been cutting off the ends of the roast—not because it improved the flavor, not because it was necessary anymore, but simply because no one had ever questioned the reason behind it. Patterns are the same: there are certain things you do that are no longer necessary or effective. Which elements of your fractal are actually no longer needed, and could be let go?

How to Change a Fractal

If changing our patterns were as simple as making a deliberate choice with our mind, it would be extraordinary. Imagine just pushing a button and instantly generating a new pattern. For example—and let me give an extreme one here—you could press the button for "velvet glove, iron fist" and suddenly embody that. Then, you press the button for "hard-working achiever," and instantly your thoughts and decisions effortlessly align with it. Next, you press the button for "rich bitch," and there it is. It would be like changing hats, effortless and instantaneous. But life doesn't work that way.

The conditioning we've received, starting from the homes we were born into, the experiences we've had, and the lessons we're meant to learn on this earthly journey, have shaped us. Having this condition has caused us to create patterns we "fight" with, patterns that govern our behavior and keep us functioning within a certain frequency.

And this is where pain comes in. Pain highlights the limitations of these patterns because we desire something beyond them. It's that yearning for change, coupled with the frustration of being stuck, that makes it hurt so much.

As much as I wish we could simply choose to shift patterns, like putting on a different outfit, that's not how it works.

So—how do you change a fractal?

To begin, let's consider the fact that a fractal, or a pattern, shows up in both the small and large aspects of our lives. The same pattern repeats itself, but if you attempt to change it on the larger scale, it's unlikely to work. Why? Because making such a change requires immense effort, including the constant, conscious attention of your mind. And that's nearly impossible to maintain.

Instead, there are 2 effective ways to change a fractal: acting on external factors, and working with internal factors. Let's take them one by one.

External Factors: Changing the Environment, Behaviors, and Habits

One way to shift a fractal is by introducing small changes in your daily environment and habits. Select a minor component of your daily routine and make a deliberate adjustment that aligns with the new pattern you want to create.

For example, if you struggle with procrastination, identify a specific area where it occurs. Let's say you procrastinate when it comes to exercise. To counter this, make exercise the very first activity of your day. Place your sneakers and training outfit beside your bed, so they're the first thing you see in the morning. Prepare your exercise equipment and your TV or tablet for guided routines in a visible and accessible spot. The moment you wake up, put on your shoes and start exercising. By repeating this consistently over time—not just for 21 days, but for a much longer period—you can reprogram your behavioral pattern. This method doesn't require deep knowledge of universal laws and is accessible to anyone willing to try.

Internal Factors: Addressing the Root Cause

The second approach involves addressing the root cause of the pattern. This method is faster and more efficient but often requires specialized skills or the guidance of a professional. The goal is to uncover and balance the underlying reasons why the pattern exists in the first place.

You start by recognizing the benefits of the pattern you want to change. It's essential to list a significant number of benefits—aim for about 100 as you will see in the next story about Rebecca. I know, I know—your brain just screamed, "A hundred? Are you serious?!" Relax—70 is still ok, and I promise this exercise isn't just a creative form of torture.

Here's why. When you're asked to give a large number of responses to the same question, the purpose is to go beyond general or surface-level answers. Those kinds of umbrella responses don't get to the root cause of the situation. For instance, if you say you work hard because "you know for sure that things are happening," that's quite broad. But that one answer can actually be broken down into 10 more precise, personal insights.

Maybe you carry the belief, "If I don't do it myself, it won't be done right"—a belief you picked up from your father, who repeated it often. That's specific. That's useful. And that's what we're aiming for.

The reason you're invited to go deep and come up with a hundred responses is because, buried in those, you'll find the truly meaningful ones. Out of the 100, maybe only 10 to

15 will speak directly to the core 20% of causes that create 80% of your current reality.

Remember—whatever your mind does, it believes it's using the most efficient strategy to get a set of results, and fulfill your top priorities. But unless you know what result it's trying to get, you can't begin to change the strategy. That's why we go deep. That's why we go specific.

Patterns don't happen by accident—they exist because they serve a purpose. For instance, procrastination might serve as a coping mechanism—it often shows up when there is a conflict between what you really want and what others expect from you. When you understand the conditioning behind the pattern, you can identify which perceptions need to be neutralized.

You're going to see how this worked for my client, Rebecca, in just a moment. Once she worked on identifying the benefits of the current pattern and uncovering the subconscious conditioning, she was able to break out of the limits of her pattern and achieve the unthinkable.

At this stage, balancing these perceptions helps dissolve the root cause, making it easier to release the pattern and replace it with a new one.

Breaking the "Working Hard" Mold

When I first met Rebecca during an online session, it was immediately evident that she embodied the "working hard" archetype. She joined the meeting right from the restaurant she owned, visibly out of breath and still wearing her apron. "I'm in a backroom of the restaurant. It's the only way I could make this session with you happen," she explained, brushing a strand of hair from her face.

That first impression said it all: Rebecca's hunched shoulders were a clear sign of the heavy load of responsibility she carried. Everything about her demeanour said, "I'm overwhelmed. I have a lot on my plate. I bear the brunt of it all. I'm not afraid of hard work. I roll up my sleeves and get the job done alongside my workers." In one of our early sessions, Rebecca confessed, "I can't keep doing this. I feel like I'm running on fumes. But every time I think about stepping back, I feel guilty, like I'm abandoning the business."

To address this, I proposed we work on her "working hard" pattern. My starting approach was to have Rebecca identify 100 perceived benefits of her "working hard" mentality, helping us uncover and dismantle its subconscious roots. As we went through it, a major realization surfaced. Rebecca shared, "When I was 7 years old, I was sent to live with my grandparents while my younger brother stayed with my parents. I always felt like I had to excel academically and work tirelessly just to get their attention."

She paused, her voice tinged with emotion. Her eyes misted over and a subtle weight seemed to press down on her shoulders as she made the connection. "I thought the only way to earn their love was to get good grades and push myself really hard. And now, I see it—I've carried this belief into adulthood. It's like I'm still trying to prove myself, even though there's no one left to prove it to," she shared quietly.

"Rebecca," I began softly, "what you're describing is a dynamic where patterns formed in childhood continue to show up in your adult life. Your hard work has likely been driven by a subconscious belief that your worth is tied to effort. But what if you saw your worth as inherent, not something you have to earn through endless toil?"

Her eyes widened. "You really think that's possible?"

"It's not just possible," I replied. "It's essential. By untangling these patterns, you can start to free yourself from the weight you've been carrying."

Over the course of several sessions, we worked through her perceptions of her parents, grandparents, and brother, addressing each memory and neutralizing its emotional charge. With every step, Rebecca began to see the connections more clearly. One day, she told me, "I started delegating tasks at the restaurant. It's strange, not being in the middle of everything, but it feels lighter—like I'm finally giving myself permission to breathe."

For the first time, she stepped away from the front lines, trusting her team to handle day-to-day operations and she focused on her role as a strategic entrepreneur, something she didn't allow herself to do before.

Two years later, Rebecca's transformation extended to another area of her life. She decided to lose weight, something she had struggled with for years. "I used to be very slim," she recalled during one session. "But since I worked nonstop and carried so much on my shoulders, I gained weight. It was like my body was mirroring the load of my life."

She chose what felt like the easiest path: stomach slimming surgery. "It was a tough decision," she admitted. "At first, it felt like I was taking the easy way out, and that didn't sit well with the old me. But the results were incredible. It proved to me that I don't have to suffer to achieve my goals anymore."

Today, Rebecca runs 3 businesses simultaneously, but her role has shifted entirely. "I'm not the one implementing or executing anymore," she explained with a smile. "I've learned to let go and trust others." The transition from sweating on the service line to strategizing as a seasoned entrepreneur marked a profound shift in her mindset. "It's a huge trans-formation," she reflected. "Not just in my businesses, but in how I see myself and my life."

Rebecca's story serves as a reminder of how deeply ingrained patterns can be unraveled and redefined—allowing us to step into a new way of being.

3 Principles of Fractals

Fractals are an intriguing concept that illustrate how you can influence systems at every level. While there are many principles related to fractals, I want to focus on the 3 that have profound implications for personal growth and systemic transformation.

1. Small Changes Create Big Results

The first principle of fractals is that small changes can lead to significant transformations because the small reflects the large. When you focus on making consistent, incremen-tal changes, the larger system naturally aligns and adapts. For instance, by addressing a small, specific habit in your life and persistently working on it, you create a ripple effect that influences the broader patterns of your behavior and circumstances. This happens because systems naturally seek internal coherence, and repeating the process at the micro level will subsequently align the macro accordingly. That's the beauty of working with fractals: by transforming the micro, you inevitably transform the macro.

2. Patterns Persist in That Form Until They Fulfill Their Purpose

The second principle is that fractals, or patterns, remain in your life in a specific form as long as they serve you. This challenges the common belief that you can simply decide to let go of something that no longer serves you. If a pattern is still present in your life, it's because it continues to fulfill a purpose, even if that purpose isn't immediately apparent. Letting go of a pattern isn't about willpower alone. It first requires understanding how it serves you, followed by transforming the internal alignment around it. You can only move beyond the pattern by fully integrating the lessons or benefits it offers.

3. Patterns Are Not Meant to Be Eliminated

The third principle emphasizes that fractals are not something you can eliminate. Instead of trying to eradicate a pattern—like procrastination—recognize its inherent function. Procrastination, for example, isn't about avoiding tasks altogether—it's about prioritizing what truly matters to you. You'll continue to delay things that aren't important, while naturally focusing on those that are. The goal isn't to stop the pattern but to work with it, understanding its purpose and adapting it to align with your priorities.

The Fractal Lesson: Changing the World One Small Act at a Time

Years ago, my best friend found himself in one of the darkest phases of his life. He believed life was meaningless. No matter what he did, he felt too small to make an impact in the world. He thought his existence was so insignificant that, if he were to vanish, life around him would carry on as though nothing had happened. This sense of futility pulled him into a deep depression.

As a child, he had big dreams. He wanted to transform society and leave a meaningful mark on the world. But as he grew older, cynicism replaced his youthful optimism. He began to think the world was immovable, unchangeable— perhaps it wasn't meant to be changed at all.

At that time, my friend was leading a nonprofit organization dedicated to promoting education for underprivileged children in rural communities. From my perspective, he was already making a difference. Yet, he didn't see it that way anymore. The weight of his despair convinced him that his efforts were futile. Even if they helped a child from a remote village get into college, what was the point? He reasoned that the world would remain the same regardless. His sense of hopelessness grew so strong that he considered shutting the organization down.

One day, he encountered the concept of fractals. His fascination began with the shell of a snail. As he studied its structure, he noticed a curious pattern: the tiny curves of the shell echoed the larger spiral as it expanded outward. This observation sparked a revelation. He realized that small patterns often replicate themselves on a grander scale. This seemingly simple insight resonated deeply with him.

He began to grasp the immense power of small actions. He saw that by making a small change early in the snail's spiral, right at the very beginning, the entire pattern would transform. Why couldn't the same idea hold true for life and society? This newfound perspective helped him see that even minor, intentional changes could lead to profound transformations. The epiphany broke through the darkness of his depression, rekindling a sense of inspiration he hadn't felt in years.

With a renewed sense of purpose, he shared his insight with his team. He spoke about fractals and how their organization's small contributions had the potential to trigger larger societal shifts. That year, they doubled in size. Together, they helped 3 times as many children gain access to quality education. Each child represented a small change of a fractal that could ripple outward into the broader world.

Let this story be a reminder. No matter how small your actions may seem, they carry the potential to create larger ripples in the world. By learning and applying the universal laws of mathematics and physics, you can train your mind to see the hidden order, where other people might only see chaos. This alone has the power to change your world and the world of those around you.

Practical Application

Here are 2 simple ways to start practicing the law of fractals into your daily life.

1. Identify a Money Pattern

Notice which symptoms repeat themselves in your relationship with money. The situations that keep happening are the clearest indicators that there's a pattern at play.

Here are a few examples:

- When you have a lot of money, does it slip through your fingers and leave you wondering where it all went?
- Is your financial life like a yo-yo—up and down, up and down—or are the events predictable?
- When you finally reach a financial goal, does the money seem to vanish—maybe through an accident or an unexpected expense?
- Has it happened more than once that you were deceived when it came to money?
- Do you feel undervalued when it comes to money? Are you underpaid and this keeps repeating, over and over again?

Take a quiet moment to reflect on what keeps repeating in your financial life, and notice the sequence of actions, emotions, and thoughts that form the pattern.

2. Choose a Recurrent Action That Can Change the Money Pattern

Find the smallest behavior you can adjust. It's important that it's an action that can be done daily or weekly and can influence the larger pattern because you are applying the law of fractals that says the way you do one thing is the way you do everything.

For example, if you're underpaid and receiving whatever others decide, one thing you can do is give yourself the first half hour of your day—non-negotiable. That's how you begin to honor yourself first. It's something you can do daily: take those 30 minutes each morning to either do nothing or enjoy your coffee in peace—but don't answer messages, don't open your phone, don't let distractions in. You're not doing anything for the kids, not for your partner, not for your job—you're doing something for you. Maybe you read, maybe you listen to music, maybe you move your body—whatever nourishes your soul.

Here's how this works: when others pay you less than you're worth, it usually means you're underestimating your own value. The world mirrors your self-perception. By starting each day by honoring yourself—before anything else—you begin to reprogram your brain. That morning time becomes your highest paycheck to yourself. With consistency, your outer world will reflect your inner shift.

So, choose a small action you can repeat daily or weekly that will impact the pattern you identified previously.

AFTERWORD

A NEW BEGINNING

If you can, close your eyes for a moment. Take a deep breath. Feel it—the weight of everything you've lived through, the moments of loss, the moments of joy, the quiet whispers of your soul guiding you all along. Can you sense it—the invisible thread that has woven every experience into the tapestry of who you are?

What if—right now—you were standing on the threshold of a choice your soul made long before you were born?

If an insight you have read in this book has touched something in you—it's because a part of you already knew. Somewhere deep inside, beyond the mind's endless questions and the heart's lingering wounds, you have always known.

You are not here by accident. This book did not find you by chance.

So—what now?

You could close these pages, move on with life, and let the insights settle into the background, another interesting idea tucked away in your mind. Or you could decide that this is the moment everything shifts. Not in a distant, vague "someday," but now, in this breath, in this heartbeat, in this life that is yours alone to live.

Maybe, for the first time, you truly understand: you are not a victim of fate. You are the creator of your reality. You always have been.

The hardships you have endured, the people who have challenged you, the love you have lost and found—all of it was chosen, by you, for you. Not as punishment, but as part of a sacred contract that your soul agreed to. It's part of your becoming, of who you're meant to be in this world—without compromises, without excuses, without making yourself small to fit in.

So the real question is not "Why did this happen to me?" but rather "What will I do with this?"

Will you keep replaying old patterns, or will you finally rewrite your story?

Will you let your fears lead, or will you step into your own power?

Will you remain a bystander in your own life, or will you fully embody the role you were always meant to play?

No more waiting. No more hoping that something out there will change. The only moment that ever truly exists is the one you're in. And in this moment, you have a choice.

Will you take full responsibility for your life and every-thing in it?

Will you meet your past—not with resistance, but with gratitude for the lessons it offered?

Will you dare to dream not only of what is possible, but also of what your soul already knows is waiting for you?

The universe is not withholding anything from you. The love, the abundance, the clarity, the peace—it is all here, right now. The only thing standing between you and the life you were born to live is the belief that something is missing.

So—what if nothing was missing? What if, right now, you already had everything you needed?

Breathe that in. Let it settle. Because the moment you truly embody it—that is the moment your reality starts to change. Not through force, not through resistance, but through a shift so profound that it echoes through every decision you make from this day forward.

This is not the end of a book. This is the beginning of a new way of being. And the only thing left to ask yourself is this: *Who will I become now that I finally start to remember who I am?*

What's Next

Thank you for being with me on this profound journey—where stories, questions, and scientific facts have woven naturally into what I hope to be a fresh new perspective for your life.

Now that you've arrived here, you might feel like you've opened a door and you want more. You're ready to continue and you're wondering what comes next. So below, I've outlined 5 pathways through which you can carry forward the energy and openness this book has offered you.

1. Continue Alongside Your FTP Specialist

If this book was recommended to you by an FTP specialist—that is, a specialist in applying universal laws to human behavior—now is a good time to send them a message. They can offer invaluable support in addressing the issues you can't resolve on your own. If you haven't done so already, identify the problem with the strongest emotional charge and work with your specialist to transform it once and for all.

2. Sign Up for the Power on Heels Program

If you are a woman who feels the time has come to rewrite your story and make a leap towards an even more authentic version of yourself, Power on Heels is the perfect program for that. It is a place of inner truth where women choose to transform their past into power, with guided steps and real emotional support over the course of 10 weeks.

Working in a group has 2 enormous advantages. First, you learn from the situations of other ladies just as much as from your own. You are not alone—the lessons of the other women are also yours. And second, the price is far more accessible than individual sessions.

If you want to find out more or need guidance to decide to what extent Power on Heels is for you, schedule a free online meeting with a program consultant from our team at the link below. I'd love to see you in the Power on Heels program and witness your next step in transformation.

InspiredLifeCircle.com/book-call-7

3. Enroll in the Inspired Money Foundation Program

If in your heart you feel that money patterns are not just about numbers, but about fears, mental programming from the past, and old family stories, then this program is for you.

Over 9 weeks, you'll work at the root of your financial issues and transform them methodically, step by step. It's an invitation to break through financial limitations and develop a healthier relationship with money—better than ever before.

You can book a free session with a program consultant and you'll sense whether it's what you need now or perhaps later.

InspiredLifeCircle.com/book-call-7

4. Join the Inspired Life Circle Community

In a world where the noise keeps getting louder, we've intentionally chosen to be less active on social media and to stay connected in a more intimate way.

Inspired Life Circle is a private community, designed to support people who are ready for accelerated growth and transformation. It's a space of support, learning, and ongoing inspiration—a living extension of this book.

Joining is currently free, but it involves a selection process and a set of guidelines that preserve the community's cohesion. That's because we want to make sure this space remains safe and meaningful for everyone involved.

Apply at InspiredLifeCircle.com—and I hope to see you soon at one of the community events, online or offline.

5. Become an FTP Specialist and Make a Living by Solving Problems with the Universal Laws

If the insights and stories you've discovered here resonate deeply and you're inspired to master the art and science of solving life's challenges through universal laws, consider attending the School of Universal Laws. Whether your goal is to become an FTP specialist and build a meaningful career in this field, or to enhance your own leadership and personal growth, this 6-month program provides a comprehensive pathway for both aspirations.

The only prerequisite for the School of Universal Laws is completing one of the foundational programs above—though you can clarify this easily in a conversation with one of my wonderful colleagues.

...

Each of these options is an invitation. A bridge between your past story and your authentic essence. Choose the path that calls to you most strongly and remember—you don't have to walk it alone.

If you feel the need for clarity, support, or simply want to talk to someone who truly understands the depth of these processes, schedule a free session with one of our program consultants. They'll be glad to walk alongside you and support you in choosing what fits best right now. You can do that now, at

InspiredLifeCircle.com/book-call-7

Carry the Light of This Book Forward

In my own life, I've come across books that touched me so deeply, I felt compelled to pass them on—as if it wasn't just about me, but about everyone who needed that message. I would buy them in packs, 10 or 15 at a time, and offer them to my friends and clients.

If *The 7 Universal Laws* touched your heart and planted a seed of transformation in you, here's a heartfelt suggestion: pass it on. Choose at least 3 people in your life who could benefit from this message, and give them the book. It might be a friend, a colleague, a sibling, or a client who needs this.

Another way to pass it on is by sharing a review on Amazon, Goodreads, or Audible. It means the world to me and Stefan. Reviews are like lanterns in the dark—illuminating the path you've just walked and inviting others to take their first step.

For you, it might be a small gesture. For them, it could be the beginning of a new path.

Thank you for choosing to be the bridge between this book and someone else's heart.

www.ingramcontent.com/pod-product-compliance
Lightning Source LLC
LaVergne TN
LVHW051727080426
835511LV00018B/2918